Lighthouses of the
CHESAPEAKE BAY

BAY BEACONS

Lighthouses
of the Chesapeake Bay

by

Linda Turbyville

EASTWIND PUBLISHING
ANNAPOLIS, MARYLAND

Published by Eastwind Publishing
Annapolis, Maryland

©1995 Eastwind Publishing
First Edition

Library of Congress Card Number: 95-60984

Turbyville, Linda
Bay Beacons
Lighthouses of The Chesapeake Bay

Includes bibliographical references and index

ISBN 1-885457-07-3

Printed in Hong Kong

Acknowledgments

First and foremost, appreciation is owed to the publisher, D. Patrick Hornberger of Eastwind Publishing. In conception and design, the following work is his alone and represents but one facet of his many years of thoughtful study of the Chesapeake Bay region—its diversity and beauty, its natural and human history.

So, too, many individuals directly involved in the historic preservation of the lighthouses of the Chesapeake Bay gave generously of their time to answer questions and offered exciting excursions through their files or out to the lighthouses of the bay: Herb Entwistle, President of the Chesapeake Chapter, U.S. Lighthouse Society; Richard Lesher, The Chesapeake Bay Maritime Museum, St. Michaels, Maryland; Richard J. Dodds, Curator of Maritime History, The Calvert Marine Museum, Solomons, Maryland; Angie Spicer VanDereedt, Archivist, Archives of the United States, Washington, D.C.; Robert Browning, Historian, U.S. Coast Guard Headquarters, Washington, D.C.; Dennis O'Brien, Director, The Living Classrooms Foundation, Baltimore, Maryland; Lieutenant John Arenstam, recently of the Office of Aids to Navigation, U.S. Coast Guard 5th District Headquarters, Portsmouth, Virginia; Colonel James M. Bosley, Deputy Commander, and Douglas Reed Macmillan, Cultural Resource Manager, Aberdeen Proving Ground, Aberdeen, Maryland; Michael Humphries, Director, St. Clement's Island-Potomac River Museum of St. Mary's County, Maryland; Orlando Rideout, The Maryland Commission to Save the Lighthouses; Boatswain's Mate First Class, Donald W. Merritt, U.S. Coast Guard ATN, St Inigoes, Maryland; and Richard Bowers, Park Manager, Elk Neck State Park. I would also like to thank Michael Bowler of *The Baltimore Sun* for the location of valuable information, and Charles A. Nomina of Staunton, Virginia, for navigational aid and invaluable research assistance. To all of the above, I apologize for those limitations that did not permit use of all the proffered material and insight.

Thanks also go to the many individuals whose professional skills and energetic activities as "lighthouse friends" are largely responsible for the preservation of so many of these historic Chesapeake Bay structures: Keith Freer, Donald Hammett and Jennifer Horton, Point Lookout State Park; Ellsworth B. Shank, Jane S. Jackstite, Joe Guzman and Elsie Stackhouse, The Friends of Concord Point Lighthouse; Jack L. Davis, The Havre de Grace Maritime Museum; Charles A. Maslin, The Battery Island Preservation Society; and Leona C. Kemper, Chairwoman, Jones Point Restoration Committee, Mount Vernon Chapter of the Daughters of the American Revolution, among many, many others. Special acknowledgment is also owed to Robert de Gast for his beautiful photographic essay, *The Lighthouses of the Chesapeake*, and to The Maryland Historical Trust for their thorough 1991 report on the condition of twelve of Maryland's twenty-three remaining lighthouses.

The author and publisher would like to thank The Enoch Pratt Library, Baltimore, Maryland, especially the help of the staff of The Maryland Room. Our thanks also go to the staff of the Mariners' Museum in Newport News, Virginia. For unswerving encouragement and dogged perseverance in seeing this book through publication, the publisher also extends grateful thanks to Nick Cannistraro.

Finally, I would like to thank the many lighthouse enthusiasts that I met and chatted with on numerous excursions along the shores and on the waters of the Chesapeake Bay. It is to you that this book is dedicated.

Contents

Preface

Those of us who love lighthouses in general, and those of the Chesapeake Bay in particular, have often started our study with Ross Holland's *America's Lighthouses* and then continued to Robert de Gast's *The Lighthouses of the Chesapeake*. For some time we have hoped for more. Now we have a major work combining beautiful color photos with well-researched text to add to our libraries. If you already love the lights of the bay, this will strengthen that love. If you are not already a lighthouse enthusiast, this volume will make you one.

As in other areas of the country, the preservation of Chesapeake Bay lighthouses has reached a point of urgency. In the past 20 years, as a growing number of individuals and organizations have sought means to preserve the lighthouses of the Chesapeake Bay, the lack of a current source of information has become critical. This book fills that gap. The Coast Guard, which has a long and admirable history as successor to the Bureau of Lighthouses in the Department of Commerce, is anxious to be relieved of the responsibility and expense of maintaining these historical structures. On the whole, we have been most fortunate in the level of care and maintenance provided by the United States 5th Coast Guard District. Increasingly however, responsibility for preserving the lights must fall to state and local groups.

Several of the lights are already being maintained by such groups, both public and private. Hooper Strait has been moved to the Chesapeake Bay Maritime Museum in St. Michaels, Drum Point has been moved to the Calvert Marine Museum at Solomons, and the Seven Foot Knoll light has been moved to Pier 5 in Baltimore Harbor. Each has been restored and is now publicly displayed, affording to one and all the opportunity to learn something about the country's seafaring past. Concord Point at Havre de Grace has long been cared for by The Friends of Concord Point Light. Cape Henry is likewise supported by a private group, the Association for the Preservation of Virginia Antiquities. Jones Point, in Alexandria, Virginia, is under the care of the National Park Service with funding provided by the Mount Vernon Chapter of the Daughters of the American Revolution. Piney Point is owned by St. Mary's County and is cared for by the St. Clement's Island-Potomac River Museum. In addition, several lights—for example, Pooles Island, Old Point Comfort, Cove Point, and Cape Henry—are on military installations, a fortuitous circumstance affording them extra protection from vandalism, if not always from slow deterioration.

There is now a Maryland Commission to Save the Lighthouses, a group which is working as an umbrella organization to preserve and protect Maryland's historic lighthouses. Additionally, under current national law, any federal agency that owns a lighthouse must keep it from further deterioration. Nevertheless, budget realities often limit how much upkeep can be done, and restoration is almost never undertaken in these circumstances.

Fortunately for lighthouse buffs, every major type of lighthouse is represented in the Chesapeake Bay: brick and stone masonry towers, houses with lanterns on the roof, screwpiles, cast-iron caissons, and skeletal steel towers of both 19th and 20th-century design. Several can be visited from shore, but many can only be seen from the water. Groups such as the Chesapeake Chapter, United States Lighthouse Society, which sponsor onshore meetings as well as cruises to regional groups of Chesapeake Bay lighthouses, help further enjoyment and knowledge about these bay treasures.

Those of us who love the lighthouses of the Chesapeake Bay are grateful to the author and publisher for this fine addition to our lighthouse libraries. Read it in leisure and then come join us in actually visiting and studying these hauntingly beautiful and historically rich structures, the jewels of Chesapeake Bay history.

Herb Entwistle
President, Chesapeake Chapter, United States Lighthouse Society

The cape on the South is called Cape Henry, in honour of our most noble Prince. The land white hilly sands like unto the Downes, and all along the shores great plentie of Pines and Firres.

Captain John Smith, The Historie of Virginia

Introduction

Most books about the Chesapeake Bay make at least one initial reference to Captain John Smith's voyages into its lovely but quixotic waters in the early 1600's. The quaint English spellings and the names of the bay's indigenous peoples which enliven Smith's descriptions of his adventurous voyages—*Sasquesahanock, Pawtuxunt, Patawomeke, Rapahanock, the Bay of Chisapeack*—pique the imagination, evoking a magical kingdom, a shimmering watery world that abounds with life, "*a plaine wildernesse,*" Smith wrote, "*as God first made it.*" The two hundred years following Smith's bold exploration of the Chesapeake saw the extraordinary growth of European settlement in the colonies of Virginia and Maryland, but one hundred and seventy-five years after Smith drew his remarkably accurate map of the Chesapeake Bay and its tributaries, there was only one lighthouse on the bay, the lighthouse at Cape Henry—a tower which remains standing today.

It is undeniable that fascination with the lighthouses of the Chesapeake Bay—and with lighthouses more generally—is growing, and the burgeoning number of lighthouse enthusiasts is in itself an interesting phenomenon to observe. It is important to note that the lighthouse is at once a powerful and a complex symbol—of safe harbor and protection from life's inclemencies, of being lost, and also, of being found, of light against darkness and despair, of rugged independence and freedom from the hassles that infect the crowded circumstances of much day-to-day living. For some, the lighthouse presents a transcendent image of perfect domesticity, for others, of romance and erotic love, while to others it suggests nothing less than withdrawal from society, perhaps to a life lived in harmony with nature—or, alternatively, to a life of heroic battle against the elements. Last of all, the lighthouse is a symbol of light against ignorance—of progress and enlightenment. These images— hope, safety, enlightenment, love—are universal human longings, emotionally charged, and often somewhat at odds with each other, and though all of them tell us something about ourselves, they tell us little about the lighthouses, of the people and the nation that built them, or the people who lived and worked in them.

In many ways, the story of the lighthouses of the Chesapeake Bay is a story of the 19th century—a time of great national energy, commercial expansion and collective optimism, a time of unprecedented immigration to the United States, and a period of both phenomenal industrial growth and of extraordinary technological innovation. These changes are reflected in the evolution of Chesapeake Bay lighthouses from squat land-hugging towers surrounded by large gardens, to trim cottages with large porches that perched gaily atop the deceptively spindly cast-iron legs with flanges screwed tightly into the soft shoals of the bay, and, finally, to stately brick Victorian townhouses with sloping mansard roofs in the open waters of the bay (lighthouses that oddly bespeak the solid stuffiness of our turn-of-the-century bourgeois). It is an architectural evolution, too, that reminds us of our country's development from rural life, to town life, to city life.

The Great Wicomico lighthouse at the mouth of the Great Wicomico River on Virginia's Western shore was dismantled in 1967. Photo 1952, Robert Lunsford, Reedville, Virginia.

But the story also dips into the 18th and now traverses almost all of the 20th century. So, too, the Chesapeake Bay lighthouses, though now eerily devoid of human occupants, strangely remind us of other important aspects of our history, and it is worth noting that many of the changes in American society that have become widespread in the latter years of the 20th century—in family life, in the increased discipline and regulation of the workplace, and, finally, in the automation of the workplace (even when we think of the information superhighway and cyberspace)—seem to have been experienced much earlier by the men and women of the lighthouse service.

First of all, it is well to bear in mind that what we today call lighthouses were at one time homes—family residences where, for at least a half a century, husbands, wives and their children (and, not infrequently, an assortment of other relatives) found the full measure of their lives together. Many of the Chesapeake Bay light stations—for example, the lights at Turkey Point and Point Lookout—were managed almost exclusively by women. Many other light stations had women on the payroll as assistant keepers, usually, but not always, the wives of keepers. But in its very first statement of personnel regulations, the Light-House Board declared that "[w]omen and servants must not be employed in the management of the lights, except by the special authority of the department." On the Chesapeake Bay, the wives and children of the keepers of screwpile lighthouses were increasingly required to live on shore, separating the man, and his performance of remunerative work, from the day-to-day, domestic activities of his wife and family. This was justified—and clearly not without reason—by the numbers of lighthouses that were swept away by winter ice floes. Additionally, the exclusion of women was justified by the growing reliance on heavy machinery, especially the machinery used to strike the fog bells. Even so, many women fought successfully to keep their jobs and the last woman lighthouse keeper in the United States was Fannie Salter, the keeper of Turkey Point light in the upper bay.

Beginning in the mid-1800's, one also traces in the story of these lighthouses and their keepers the outlines of important changes, yet to come, in the whole tone and temper of the American workplace. The establishment of the Light-House Board in the 1850's, for example, which took upon itself the work of reshaping the United States light service—then renowned as "one of the worst in the world"— into the world's best, provides a truly classic study in the growth of 19th-century bureaucracy and foreshadows in many ways, especially in the strict allotment of tools, supplies, and tasks, the strategies of scientific management which were adopted by American industry at the turn of the century. The hierarchical organization of the Board, the standardization of procedure and the strict codification of keepers' duties anticipate the spreading discipline and the increasingly authoritarian regulation of working life in American society as a whole.

Of great interest, too, and highly visible in the development of lighting apparatuses and fog signals as well as in telephone, radio and radar communications, is American society's love affair with innovative technology—including its ready acceptance of and willingness (in fact, eagerness) to rely on mechanized equipment.

And, finally, beginning in earnest right after the First World War, one finds the repudiation of human labor in favor of a fully-automated service, and one observes the slow but steady retirement of lighthouse keepers, also previewing, in many ways, the shift from skilled labor to robotics which has so characterized industrial development during the latter years of this century.

Two coastguardsmen maintained the fourth-order fresnel lens in the Great Wicomico lighthouse. Photo, 1952, Robert Lunsford, Reedville, Virginia.

As the history of the Cape Henry light shows, the British colonial government proved remarkably inefficient with regard to the need for reliable navigational aids in the colonies, and nowhere was this bureaucratic ineptitude (and probable indifference) more apparent than along the much-traveled maritime routes through the Virginia Capes into the complex waterways and often shallow waters and shifting shoals of the 200-mile-long Chesapeake Bay. On the western shore, it's major navigable tributaries include the James, York, and Rappahannock rivers in Virginia, and the Potomac, Patuxent, and Patapsco rivers in Maryland as well as the mouth of the Susquehanna River which tumbles down from the mountainous regions of Pennsylvania (and is rightly called the mother of the Chesapeake Bay). On the eastern shore the Chester, Choptank, Wicomico and Nanticoke rivers, all of them navigable, were also the site of much colonial shipping, most especially that which was occasioned by the proliferation of plantation tobacco growers. During the 18th (and well into the 19th century), the Chesapeake Bay enjoyed the highest volume of commercial shipping in North America and thus the failure of the British colonial government to provide for the safety of maritime traffic in and out of the bay was all the more disturbing. Although the major shoals were marked by buoys, the movement of ice through the bay in the winter as well as the deliberate actions of pirates who hoped to profit from an arranged shipwreck, occasioned the frequent rearrangement of these buoys and occasioned many maritime disasters.

In August of 1789, the newly formed federal government of the United States was not about to abandon its treasury to the vagaries of wind and weather. Acutely aware of the economic importance of its international trade, a commerce that of course relied entirely on shipping, the ninth law passed by the First Congress assumed jurisdiction over all then existing navigational aids.[1] At the same time, Congress directed attention to the prompt completion of the Cape Henry light and the Virginia assembly lost no time in ceding

[1]There were no more than a handful, including eight to twelve beacons requiring keepers: 1) Portsmouth Harbor light (1771); 2) Boston light (1716); 3) Gurnet Point lights—or Plymouth light (1769); 4) Brant Point light (1746); 5) Beaver Tail light (1749); 6) Sandy Hook light (1764); 7) Cape Henlopen light (1767); 8) Charleston Main light—or Morris Island light (1767); 9) Portsmouth light (1771); 10) New London light (1760); 11) Tybee Island light (1748); and 12) Cape Ann light (1771). One hundred years later the United States had 672 lighthouses and 32 light vessels in service. Additionally, there were 1,920 other lighted aids and 5,151 fog signals and unlighted buoys.

the parcel of land at Cape Henry to the federal government.[2] An appropriation for the construction was secured in 1791 and the light—the first to be completed under the auspices of the federal government—was commissioned the following year.

The fledgling United States government's awareness of the economic importance of lighthouses, beacons and daymarks, and its relatively generous appropriations for the construction of lighthouses did not, however, translate immediately into the creation of an effective lighthouse service. Initially, the navigational aids were placed under the direction of the Secretary of the Treasury, Alexander Hamilton, where they remained for approximately three years. Next they were transferred to the newly created Office of Commissioner of Revenue—an office that was abolished ten years later, once again returning navigational aids to the direct jurisdiction of the Secretary of the Treasury. Albert Gallatin, Secretary of the Treasury from 1801 until 1814, was particularly interested in maritime matters and was active in pushing Congress to make appropriations for new lighthouses. But the same cycle was repeated one more time—an Office of Commissioner of Revenue was established that took charge of navigational aids and then, seven years later, was once again abolished. Although approximately 40 lighthouses were built during the early federal period, only a few still survive—in fact, most were gone before the outbreak of the Civil War. One of the few survivors is the old Cape Henry lighthouse, condemned in 1881 when it was replaced with a new lighthouse, but, remarkably, still standing today.

In 1820, the lights were placed under the superintendence of the Fifth Auditor of the Treasury, a tentative but nonetheless important first step in the consolidation of the lighthouse service. Before navigational aids were remanded to the Fifth Auditor, the lack of any clear delineation of administrative authority meant that the resolution of even the minutiae of lighthouse operation—for example, the purchase of oil or the appointment of keepers— often reached the desk of the president of the United States. (In fact, the signatures of Presidents Washington and Jefferson can be found on many early lighthouse documents.) But, as is so often the case, the administrative cure produced some unfortunate side effects: too much decision-making authority was placed in the hands of the Fifth Auditor, Stephen Pleasanton, a tightwad with no appreciable experience in matters of lighthouse administration and the emergent "villain," one U.S. Coast Guard historian has written with apparent amusement, "of the Camelot-like history of early lighthouse construction."[3]

Under the administration of the Fifth Auditor, Chesapeake Bay lighthouse construction began in earnest and it is fair to say that the modest appearance of the Chesapeake Bay's early lighthouses has much to do with the nature of Pleasanton's administration, if not his personality. "The Fifth Auditor prided

Even at mid-century, the keeper at the Great Wicomico light kept the fog bell winding machinery in perfect working order. Photo 1952, Robert Lunsford, Reedville, Virginia.

---

[2] The deed reads, "...[T]wo acres in the county of Princess Ann, the headland of Cape Henry, with a reservation of fishing rights and the hauling of seines," and is dated November 13, 1789.

[3] Robert L. Scheina, "The Evolution of the Lighthouse Tower," *Lighthouses: Then and Now*, a supplement of the Commandant's Bulletin, U.S. Coast Guard, Washington, D.C., 1987. "After all," Scheina adds, "one would hardly expect to find a philanthropist in the Treasury Department."

himself for many years that he was able to return funds appropriated for the construction and repair of lighthouses to the Treasury unspent. ...[He] was a lighthouse novice when assigned the task and did little to improve his knowledge of lighthouse technology during his 32-year tenure."[4] Pleasanton invariably saw to it that construction contracts were awarded to the lowest bidder with the result that inferior plans and cheap materials often went into the construction of new lights and the repair of old ones.[5]

Additionally, Pleasanton maintained a very close relationship with Winslow Lewis, a former ship's captain who had contracted with the United States government in 1812 to outfit all lighthouses with his patented reflecting apparatus. The Fifth Auditor's lack of lighthouse expertise led him to consult Lewis on the technical aspects of lighthouse construction and maintenance and, in return, Pleasanton supported the continued use of Lewis's parabolic reflectors long after they had clearly been superseded by the development of Augustin Fresnel's prismatic lens. Lewis was also awarded more than one contract for lighthouse construction and it has been suggested that he was allowed to bid on some contracts after he himself had written the specifications.[6]

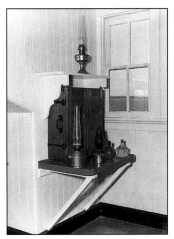

Kerosene lamps were kept on hand as emergency backup for failed electricity at the Great Wicomico light. Photo 1952, Robert Lunsford, Reedville, Virginia.

Of necessity, all of the lighthouses on the Chesapeake Bay were initially constructed on land, and John Donahoo, a town commissioner in the city of Havre de Grace and a business associate of Winslow Lewis, was the contractor who most consistently presented Pleasanton with the lowest bid. Donahoo's first lighthouse was built on Thomas Point. The tower lasted less than 15 years (when it was rebuilt by Winslow Lewis), but Donahoo's construction improved with experience so that, unlike the majority of lighthouses built during Pleasanton's term as Fifth Auditor, many of Donahoo's Chesapeake Bay lighthouses are still standing today and are discussed in the following pages: Turkey Point, Concord Point, Fishing Battery, Pooles Island, Cove Point, Piney Point and Point Lookout.

The overall vitality of 19th-century commerce on the Chesapeake Bay is perhaps best demonstrated by the number of lighthouses built between 1824 and 1908. Because of the convoluted shoreline of the Chesapeake Bay— more than 4,000 miles, plus another 4,000 if one counts the 45 noteworthy tributaries that spill fresh water into the bay—the number of active Chesapeake Bay lighthouses eventually reached almost 75. Only 34 of these lighthouses remain standing today, though, remarkably, 23 of them are still active navigational aids. Another two—Fort Carroll and Cedar Point—are so badly deteriorated that they can no longer rightly be considered as historical structures.[7]

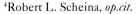

[4]Robert L. Scheina, *op.cit.*

[5]It is of interest to note that in 1825 "showing a false light" was made a felony, punishable by fine, imprisonment and confinement to hard labor.

[6]Francis Ross Holland, Jr., *America's Lighthouses*, 1972. Holland points out that Lewis was not the worst person that Pleasanton could have turned to as an advisor: "Lewis did have considerable practical maritime experience and he was gaining technical knowledge, not only through supplying the illuminating apparatuses, but also by the construction of some of the lighthouses."

[7]We have also omitted any consideration of Lazaretto Point which is a replica of a Donahoo lighthouse demolished in the 1930's.

Last but not least, one of the 34 lighthouses discussed in the following pages is Chesapeake Light—built in 1964—a lighthouse that at first glance may seem both structurally and technologically a horse of a very different color. In important ways, however, Chesapeake Light represents the endpoint of lighthouse construction, meaning the endpoint of structures built to be manned. In its design and operation, final solutions to the problems of transportation to and from shore, to communication and to keepers' living arrangements were tried—including a helicopter landing pad as well as extensive living quarters and recreational facilities for its keepers. Today, as dusk falls on Virginia Beach and Chesapeake Light begins its familiar grouped flashes on the distant horizon of restless mauve-colored waves, many local inhabitants will tell you that it is the last manned lighthouse in the United States. For these people—and perhaps in some ways for all lighthouse enthusiasts—a certain comfort, difficult to dislodge, resides in the long-observed association between the lighthouse and its keeper.

The rooftop lantern lighthouse located at Point Lookout, Maryland was home to at least three female lighthouse keepers. It is believed to be haunted by the spirits of past keepers and Civil War soldiers who died in a nearby prisoner-of-war camp. Photo (c.1855), National Archives.

Besides storms and occasional heavy winter ice, shoals were—and still are—the major obstacle to safe navigation in the Chesapeake Bay. It was for this reason that, in 1820, the Chesapeake Bay received the first U.S. lightship placed in service by the United States government. For one year, the 70-ton lightship tossed in the exposed waters at Willoughby Spit in Virginia, but the location proved too dangerous and it was moved the following year to Craney Island in the vicinity of Norfolk. At that time, four additional lightships were placed in service on the bay, and the number increased, especially following the Civil War when many lighthouses were destroyed by Confederate troops.[8] In the same manner that many of the Chesapeake Bay's land-based lighthouses were replaced by screwpile lights that could be situated farther out on treacherous shoals, improving both the visibility of their lights and the audibility of their fog signals during bad weather, so, too, many open-water lightships were replaced by sturdy caisson structures. Beginning around 1850, the advent of significant steamship traffic also greatly increased the need for reliable beacons along the deeper shipping channels, for these ships tended to pick up considerable speed in the relatively protected waters of the Chesapeake Bay.

One of the great satisfactions afforded the student of the lighthouses of the Chesapeake Bay is the opportunity to study all the major structural and architectural innovations and solutions to problems of manned lighthouse construction. In fact, the Chesapeake Bay contains numerous examples of each type of lighthouse: the stone or masonry tower and, sometimes still, the accompanying keeper's cottage (Old Point Comfort, Turkey Point, Cove Point, among others), the sturdy house—frame or brick—with a rooftop lantern (Point Lookout, Jones Point and Fishing Battery lights), the screwpile, topped with either a cast-iron or clapboard dwelling (Seven Foot Knoll, Drum Point, Hooper Strait and Thomas Point), the cast-iron cement-filled caisson, often pneumatically sunk—sometimes to great depth—beneath the mudline of the bay, affording the sturdiest solution for much-needed navigational aids in the

[8]In fact, as late as 1955, there were nine lightships positioned around the Chesapeake Bay.

open waters of the bay, topped with a conical iron tower (Thimble Shoal, Bloody Point Bar and Sharps Island, for example) or a brick masonry dwelling (Wolf Trap, Point No Point, and Sandy Point, among others), and, finally, an assortment of iron and steel skeletal towers (Craighill Channel—rear lights, both ranges, and the aforementioned Chesapeake Light). Additionally, there is the cast-iron new Cape Henry light tower and, quite an anomaly in beacon construction (or, better said, an excuse for no construction), the light on the old fog bell tower at Fort Washington.

As already noted, most of the land-based towers that dot the shores of the Chesapeake Bay were built under the administration of the Fifth Auditor, Stephen Pleasanton, a man of neither aesthetic nor architectural yearnings and one whose utter fiscal pragmatism afforded no room for the conception of a lighthouse as a civic or national monument. Nevertheless, Pleasanton did move fairly rapidly to provide navigational aids to mariners on the bay. Thus, the towers built and outfitted by John Donahoo and his associate Winslow Lewis may be taken as fairly typical of construction on the Chesapeake Bay, if only because they were responsible for the design, the choice of building materials, and the lanterns and scant appurtenances of so many of these structures.[9]

Constructed of cut stone or brick, the masonry tower is generally about 30 feet in height and assumes the shape of a truncated cone, decreasing from a diameter of 18 to 20 feet at its base to nine or ten feet at the top. The tower supports the lantern and the lantern deck, which is cantilevered a few inches beyond the top of the tower. The lantern floor is either stone, radially laid cast iron, or even a single piece of cast iron, and the lantern gallery or widow's walk is reached through a cast-iron half-door. The lantern itself, supported by masonry walls, may also be cast all of a piece in iron and the storm panel frames and fasteners are also of cast iron. The lantern is usually octagonal, the panes may be triangular or rectangular. A cast-iron balustrade surrounds the cat walk. Adjustable brass ventilators are set into the masonry of the lantern walls and the sheet metal roof sports a large brass ventilator ball and a lightning conductor. Stairwell treads follow the exterior wall of the tower and a central wooden pole; they may be iron, cut stone or wooden. The spiral stairway leads to a platform about three-quarters of the way up which served as a nighttime watch area for the keeper (a rather small area at the top of a steep stairwell which could not have been a very comfortable spot to spend the night). Usually an iron ship's ladder provides access into the lantern through an iron trap door. Two to four windows allow light to enter the interior of the tower during the day.

The keeper's cottage was often a single story or a one-and-a-half story masonry dwelling, offering a small living room, and one or two bedrooms. Each room had a closet and fireplace. The house had an attached kitchen and—sometimes, but not always—a porch. On the immediate grounds were a well and brick-lined privy. These houses were Spartan and most of the

Lighthouse keeper Fannie Salter raised the flag every day for 22 years at the masonry tower lighthouse at Turkey Point on Maryland's Elk river. She was the last civilian woman light-keeper in the U.S. when she retired in 1947. Photo (c.1930), National Archives.

[9]It is believed—and probably certain—that the old Cape Henry light followed the architectural plans and drawings of the British colonial government. A man named Elzy Burroughs built both the Old and New Point Comfort lights. All of these rather more elegant lighthouse towers predate the Fifth Auditor's assumption of the responsibilities of providing the United States with reliable maritime aids.

original cottages received considerable attention in the latter years of the 19th century. An additional story was added, increasing the living space for the keeper and his family, porches were built and enlarged, walkways were laid between the buildings and to the lighthouse proper, and the house and gardens were surrounded by picket fencing. A fog bell house was also usually built as well as other outbuildings—stables, oil house, and storage for the growing inventory of tools and equipment needed in lighthouse keeping.

Beginning in the late 1700's, the screwpile lighthouse evolved in England from lighthouse structures supported by strong substructures of wooden piles. In 1830, a British engineer, Alexander Mitchell, gave another twist, so to speak, to this design when he patented his cast-iron screwpile. Named for the broad spiraled flanges which allowed the cast-iron mooring to be screwed into a muddy river bottom or soft sand, his iron substructure proved remarkably resilient. Lighthouses with screwpile moorings were soon built on the Wyre and Thames rivers, the latter completed in 1841. By 1842, an engineer to the United States Lighthouse Survey had made note of the effectiveness of the design: "The use of screw moorings are yet unknown in this country," he wrote, "while England has availed herself of this valuable invention . . .as a means of founding lighthouses upon shoals hitherto considered inaccessible to the engineer."[10]

This screwpile lighthouse on the Choptank River off Benoni Point was originally located 100 miles south at Cherrystone Bar, Virginia. It was towed to the sight in 1921 and dismantled in 1964. Photo (c.1950), U.S. Coast Guard.

Although the first screwpile lighthouse built in the United States was located on Brandywine shoal in the Delaware Bay, it was, in fact, the Chesapeake Bay that became the site of most early screwpile construction. Because of the extensive shoals of the Chesapeake Bay, many land-based towers were of limited utility to mariners and, in heavily trafficked locations where such shoals threatened navigational safety, lightships (expensive to build and man) had been placed in service. The screwpile lighthouse was soon embraced by the Light-House Board as a relatively inexpensive solution to the navigational difficulties of the bay and approximately 42 screwpile structures were built on the Chesapeake Bay in the latter half of the 19th century. The first, commissioned in 1854, was on the Pungoteague River. Unfortunately, for want of an icebreaker, it was shorn from its foundation only two years later—foreshadowing the fate of many later structures. The second, commissioned in 1855, was Seven Foot Knoll, a lighthouse which differed from later screwpile designs in that the keeper's cottage was also constructed of cast iron.[11] In all screwpile construction, the ease of setting the foundation and the use of prefabricated parts meant that assembly was both quick (approximately one month from start to finish) and cost-effective.

The screwpile moorings usually consist of six to eight peripheral cast-iron piles and one central pile, all with auger-like flanges that are bored tightly into the bottom of the bay. These primary piles are then leveled and braced with additional rolled-iron bars and another level of structural cast-iron posts, forming a spidery but broad load-bearing infrastructure (often compared to the moon-landing vehicle in appearance) that supports the iron beams which,

[10]I.W.P Lewis, Esq. quoted in, Layne Bergin, "Screwpile Lighthouses: From Britain to the Bay," *The Keeper's Log*, Summer, 1987.

[11]Thus, in important ways, Seven Foot Knoll offered a prototype for the cast-iron caisson towers which were placed in the open waters of the bay towards the end of the century.

in turn, support the relatively lightweight timber-framed keeper's dwelling and lantern. Beneath the first level is a loading platform (where some lightkeepers kept barnyard animals) and from this level, iron ship's ladders led through a trap door to the main deck.

The Chesapeake Bay screwpile dwelling—in many ways, the signature lighthouse of the bay—was most often a charming but cozy two-story clapboard cottage of either hexagonal or octagonal design, with two to six dormer windows, a large porch deck surrounded by a wooden handrail and balustrades, and a seam metal roof, usually tin, that supported the timber-framed lantern and a lantern deck with wooden handrails and balustrades identical to those on the first level. The storm panels were framed with cast-iron mullions which supported the metal roof capped with a ventilator ball and lightning rod. Most of the screwpile lights on the Chesapeake Bay were outfitted with fourth or fifth-level Fresnel lenses.

The interior rooms of the lighthouse were finished with tongue-and-groove beaded board, usually painted white, and brightly varnished wooden floors. The first floor contained a sitting room, bedroom, storeroom and small kitchen. Cisterns, sometimes enclosed in cupboards, were used to collect rain water from the roof for the use of the keeper and his family. (Not surprisingly, an important feature of open-water lighthouse keeping was frequent roof washing.) A privy was cantilevered from the main deck.

The last major development in lighthouse construction on the Chesapeake Bay is the cast-iron caisson. In all, twelve caisson lighthouses were built on the bay between 1873 and 1914 and all are still standing and are used to exhibit active navigational aids. Most of the caisson lighthouses are located in the open waters of the bay and many cannot be seen from shore. (There are some exceptions, however: for example, Sandy Point, at the foot of the Chesapeake Bay bridge, and Newport News Middle Ground, in Hampton Roads, Virginia, one of the busiest shipping channels in the world).

Although caisson lighthouse superstructures varied somewhat in material and design, the substructure of the caisson was fairly standard. Basically the caisson is a hollow cast-iron cylinder with a diameter of approximately 30 feet and a variable height (the overall height of the foundation pier was dictated by the nature of the underlying composition of the floor of the bay). Its flanged cast-iron parts were prefabricated, numbered for ease of assembly, and then shipped to a lighthouse buoy station where the parts were bolted together. Air-tight and water-tight, the cylinder was then towed to the selected site to be sunk into the substratum of the bay and filled with a mixture of heavy stone and concrete.

Because of the enormous weight of the caisson, a careful study of the soil substratum was of the first importance. Sometimes the caisson was easily grounded by its own weight, in other instances extensive dredging was required, and in still other instances, the foundation pier needed an underlying caisson of timber piling to secure the load at a deeper level. Sometimes the caisson had to be suspended from a barge to prevent it from sinking too quickly on its own. In all instances, great care was taken to ensure that the caisson had a level bearing and that all subsequent courses were perpendicular so that the top course would be "on a true horizon line."

The cast-iron caisson lighthouse at Sharp's Island at the mouth of the Choptank River is still standing albeit listing at 15 degrees from ice movement. It replaced the previous screwpile lighthouse which fell victim to the bay's winter ice. Photo (c. 1955), collection Patrick Hornberger.

The superstructure—the dwelling and lantern—of the caisson lighthouse was often either a conical tower, built of cast-iron flanges bolted on the inside to create a smooth exterior surface, or a glazed brick masonry lighthouse with a timber-framed third level and sloping mansard roof. The cast-iron towers were the most functional in design, though most of them sport a bit of decorative ironwork around the windows or doorways. In either case, the interior walls were lined with brick and the first level of the dwelling almost surely included a sitting room, a kitchen and a storage room. In most instances, a second level was used for sleeping quarters and often a third level was built as a watch room for the on-duty keeper.

The interior rooms were finished with tongue-and-groove beaded board, and the under floor could be rough-cut timber set into the masonry or radially laid cast-iron flanges bolted together to form a smooth ceiling below and supported by the exterior iron work and perhaps a central pole. The interior stairways, of either wood or metal, were often set into the masonry of the interior wall or followed the central pole of the iron house. The lantern and gallery decks were concrete and fitted with iron balustrades and handrails, and on the second or third-level roof a fog bell was attached. The lantern was cast iron and often octagonal with a sloping metal roof, brass ventilator ball and lightning rod. In spite of their strong resemblance to turn-of-the-century city townhomes, however, few, if any, of these stout dwellings were ever family homes (unlike the screwpile lighthouses on the bay), at least not for more than a few weeks of vacation for wives and children during the summer months.

The Point No Point lighthouse is typical of the brick and masonry dwelling built on a cast-iron, cement-filled caisson. This strong construction method accounts for the survival of all of the caisson lights on the bay. Photo (c.1960), U.S. Coast Guard.

In stark contrast to the conservative practices of the Fifth Auditor, the Light-House Board embraced new technology with a will (and more than a little puffed-up pride) and commissioned reports on every tool and accessory of the lighthouse proper and the keeper's equipment—from tripoli powder to dustcloths, from wicks to lard oil, from foghorns to telephones. For the most part, the board's members were professional scientists, engineers and military men, thoroughly abreast of the technological opportunities that steam, internal combustion engines, electricity, telephone and radio afforded, and determined, as well, to find the means to bend these innovations into useful equipment and accoutrements for the lighthouse service of the United States.[12] Many of these studies, compiled in appendices to their annual reports, describe lengthy, often cumbersome experiments, but the spirit of optimism—expressed in the staunch assurance that they would find a solution for every obstacle or eventuality that might dim a light or make a foghorn inaudible—is unmistakable, and, in its own way, charming. "The theory of coast lighting," wrote one member of the Light-House Board, "is that each coast shall be so set with towers that the rays from their lights shall meet and pass each other, so that a vessel on the coast shall never be out of sight of a light, and that there shall be no dark spaces between lights.[13]

[12]The head of the Smithsonian Institution, Professor Henry James, was chairman of the Light-House Board for its first seven years.

[13]From a paper read by Edward P. Adams, member of the Boston Society of Civil Engineers, January 25, 1893, in which he quotes Johnson's "The Modern Light-House Service," a publication of the Light-House Board.

The numerous research undertakings of the Light-House Board are well documented in their annual reports and, over the years, the lighthouses and lightships of the Chesapeake Bay figured in many experiments of the Light-House Board, and later, The Bureau of Lighthouses. At Cape Charles, beginning in 1902, experiments were conducted with electrically operated fog signals—at this time, still actually bells with strikers. But perhaps the most memorable experiment with fog equipment on the Chesapeake Bay was set up at the Baltimore buoy depot in 1921. It was a fog bell that had been designed with an automatic starting device and its sensor was made of human hair. The hair, inserted into the controlling mechanism of a hygroscope, tightened and lengthened in response to air moisture. It was hoped that the device would distinguish between fog, high humidity and other moisture, but it failed this very crucial test when at nearby Fort McHenry, on the occasion of the unveiling of the Frances Scott Key Memorial, "the device," as related by Hans Christian Adamson, "called unscheduled attention to itself..."

The small framed wooden tower at Fort Washington on the Potomac River represents the simplest form of lighthouse structure on the bay's waters. It was originally built to house the fog bell and later took in the light itself. The keeper's house was nearby. Photo (c.1950), U.S. Coast Guard.

> *It was a warm and sunny summer day. President Harding was paying tribute to the genius of the author of our national anthem when out of the blue and into the attentive silence came the strident clanging of a super fog bell. It did not take long to learn that the din came from the new experimental fog signal at the Baltimore Depot of the Lighthouse Service. But the cause of the din was not revealed until some bright lad recalled that, as part of the dedication program, fire boats of the city of Baltimore had been making a spectacular display by shooting vertical streams of water high into the air from their pressure hoses.[14]*

By 1910, when the Light-House Board was dismantled and administration of aids to navigation was transferred to the Department of Commerce (becoming the Bureau of Lighthouses), U.S. law already mandated that all ships carrying more than 50 passengers be outfitted with wireless equipment. Experimentation with radio beacons began in the 1920's, and although there was much initial resistance to their use by ship captains long accustomed to relying on their ears and lead-lines during periods of reduced visibility, the accurate readings that radio beams gave to navigators eventually won the faith of all. By 1923 radio fog signals were installed on the Cape Charles Lightship and at Cape Henry light, and, in 1929, the first tests of the long-range radiobeacon direction finder (RDF) were conducted at the Cape Henry light station.[15] Within months the new system had been placed in commission and its success was astonishing. In the fifteen years between 1920 and 1935, the United States rose from sixth to second in safety of shipping, outranked only by Holland in maritime security.[16]

[14]Hans Christian Adamson's *Keepers of the Lights*, 1955 is a witty, highly readable and informative overview of the United States' lighthouse service, from its inception through the mid-1950's.

[15]Some of the first experimental radio beacons were installed at Smith Point, Wolf Trap and Cove Point in the Chesapeake Bay.

[16]Hans Christian Adamson, *op.cit.* Adamson reports that Coast Guard surveys show the extraordinary success of RDF and reports some statistics from the Great Lakes. "From 1923 to 1926, before RDF..., there were 76 strandings out of 572 vessels, or one stranding for each 7.5 vessels. From 1927 to 1930, after RDF on the lakes, there were 31 strandings out of a group of 470 vessels, or a reduction to one stranding out of each 15 vessels."

The first commissioner of the Lighthouse Bureau was George R. Putnam, formerly of the U.S. Coast and Geodetic Survey, a man who directed the service for 25 productive years. "George Putnam, " Adamson writes, "set an example of devotion to duty that percolated through the entire organization."[17] Maritime safety, largely due to the introduction of radio technology, improved greatly during his tenure as commissioner. Beloved by his employees, for whom he acquired full federal pension benefits, Putnam was also a penny-pinching administrator with the result that the Bureau of Lighthouses did not lavish the kind of care on lighthouse properties that had characterized its predecessor.

Windmill Point lighthouse once guarded the mouth of Virginia's Rappahannock River, replacing a lightship which was destroyed by Confederate troops in 1861. The screwpile lighthouse was dismantled in 1965 to be re-placed by an unattended skeletal tower. Photo (c.1950), U.S. Coast Guard.

Nevertheless, both the Bureau of Lighthouses and the Department of Navy were astonished when President Franklin D. Roosevelt placed navigational aids under the jurisdiction of the U.S. Coast Guard in the summer of 1939. Ironically, it was the summer that the lighthouse establishment was preparing to celebrate 150 years of service and *The Baltimore Sun* took note of the fact that the celebration was rapidly assuming the dimensions of a "funeral." Shortly before the transfer of navigational aids to the Coast Guard, the lighthouse commissioner, Harold D. King, looked back at the improvements made to navigational aids on the Chesapeake Bay in an address given to members of Baltimore's Propeller Club. "Progress in the Lighthouse Service," King said,

> *is not spectacular, not as a rule headline material, but let us glance back to my first cruise on the Chesapeake Bay in 1902. There was one lighted buoy between Baltimore and the Capes, now there are 185 in the Chesapeake Bay area. Then 95 percent of the buoys were wooden spars. Today less than half of them. Lightships showed lights of 4,000 candlepower. Today their candlepower is 16,000 and the lights are higher above the sea. The brightest light was Cape Charles of 130,000 candlepower. Now it is 740,000. A few of the bay lights were of 2,500 candlepower or over but most were below 500 candles. Today there are 30 ranging from 2,500 to 35,000. In 1902 radio was undreamed of. Today there are five radio beacons in the bay, all synchronized with improved fog signals for distance finding.*

Other changes had taken place as well. Only one woman remained as a keeper on Chesapeake Bay (or, for that matter, in the whole lighthouse service) and she was soon to retire.

It has now been well over 50 years since the U.S. Coast Guard assumed jurisdiction over aids to navigation. The intervening years have seen the end of manned lighthouse operation as it lives on in the hearts and minds of so many, but it is important to remember that the process of automation was initiated well before the Coast Guard assumed the helm of lighthouse administration.

Today's Coast Guard, beleaguered by an ever-growing list of responsibilities for the safety of people in the United States' coastal waters and the protection of resources along our shorelines, has neither adequate manpower nor money for the maintenance of historic lighthouse dwellings, though—it is probably a safe bet—many might prefer the prideful days of manned light-

[17]Hans Christian Adamson, *op.cit.*

house operation to the current dangers of drug-smuggling interdictment and immigration control.

According to the U.S. Coast Guard's own inspection reports, the condition of many Chesapeake Bay lighthouses is poor—even, in some instances, grim. When fully automated, the open-water lighthouses quickly became the targets of seafaring vandals. Doors and windows were broken and their decks and rooms often became nesting sites for birds. Water generally entered the first level, ruining the interior walls and flooring. Shots were fired at the lanterns, shattering storm panels and irreplaceable Fresnel lenses. Concrete decks crumbled and roofs leaked. Acrylic panes and bricked in windows, installed by the Coast Guard in an effort to secure the lighthouses, prevented ventilation of the interior structure, furthering deterioration. No longer used as living quarters, the rigorous and immaculate care which was the standard of both civilian and Coast Guard lighthouse keeping soon became an anachronism. It is perhaps worth noting that today, the shortest definition in the U.S. Coast Guard *Light List's* "Glossary of Aids to Navigation Terms" is reserved for the lighthouse—a definition that in its unadorned brevity speaks volumes. "Lighthouse. A lighted beacon of major importance."

Nevertheless, it is also important to realize that what protection and refurbishment the 23 still-active lighthouses of the bay have received in recent years is due, in no small part, to the efforts of those officers and enlisted men who do take an interest in the historical value of the lighthouses in their charge. Many small battles have been waged on behalf of Chesapeake Bay lighthouses by individuals assigned to the U.S. 5th District Coast Guard, and, in many instances, expensive repairs—and even some restoration—have been undertaken and successfully completed. On the whole, there has been a growing sensibility with respect to the need to maintain the overall historical integrity of lighthouse structures.

The cottage structure on Cedar Point at the entrance to the Patuxent River was originally built on land and later surrounded by the waters of the bay. Its construction exemplifies an era when many lighthouses were fully equipped stations with complete home-like accomodations for the keeper and his family. Photo (c.1950), U.S. Coast Guard.

Notice

This book is not intended to be used for navigation. The characteristics of any lighthouse (its range of light, fog signal or other navigational aids) are for general information only. For current information on aids to navigation of the Chesapeake Bay, please refer to navigational charts available from the U.S. National Oceanic and Atmospheric Administration. The lighthouses are listed in a north to south direction for editorial reasons only and have no relation to navigation of the Chesapeake Bay.

Ford Model A truck used by the U.S. Lighthouse Service in 1916 at the Portsmouth, Virginia depot. Photo 1916, National Archives.

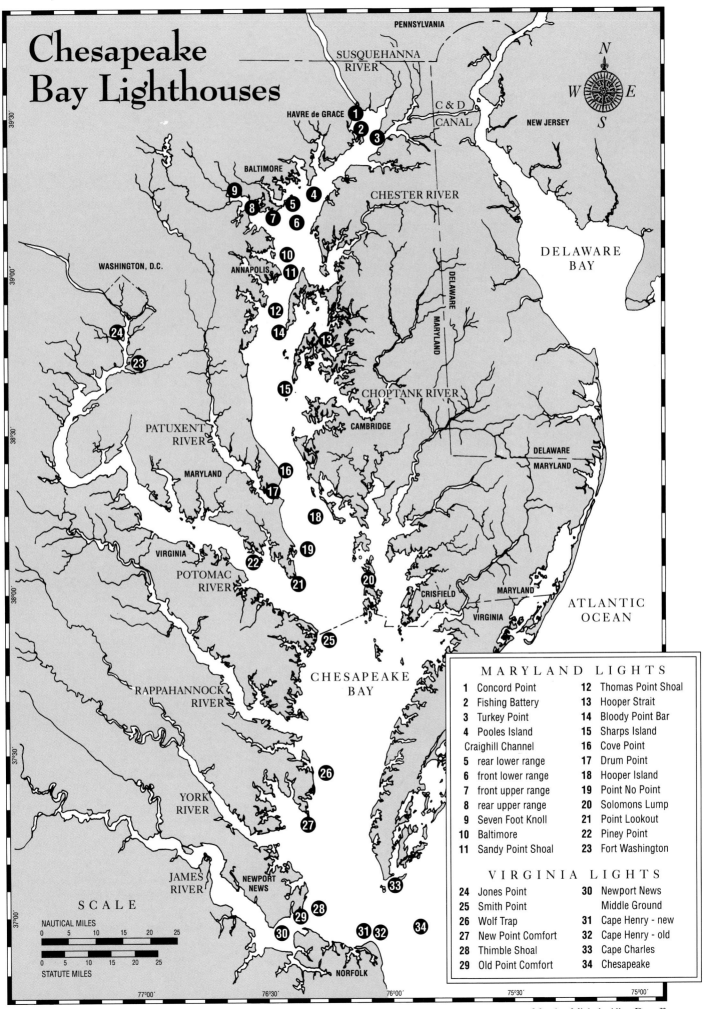

Chesapeake Bay Lighthouses

PENNSYLVANIA

SUSQUEHANNA RIVER

HAVRE de GRACE

C & D CANAL

NEW JERSEY

BALTIMORE

CHESTER RIVER

DELAWARE BAY

WASHINGTON, D.C.

ANNAPOLIS

DELAWARE

MARYLAND

CHOPTANK RIVER

CAMBRIDGE

DELAWARE

MARYLAND

PATUXENT RIVER

MARYLAND

CRISFIELD

MARYLAND

VIRGINIA

ATLANTIC OCEAN

VIRGINIA

POTOMAC RIVER

CHESAPEAKE BAY

RAPPAHANNOCK RIVER

YORK RIVER

JAMES RIVER

Newport News

NORFOLK

SCALE

NAUTICAL MILES

0   5   10   15   20   25

STATUTE MILES

0   5   10   15   20   25

MARYLAND LIGHTS	
1 Concord Point	**12** Thomas Point Shoal
2 Fishing Battery	**13** Hooper Strait
3 Turkey Point	**14** Bloody Point Bar
4 Pooles Island	**15** Sharps Island
Craighill Channel	**16** Cove Point
5 rear lower range	**17** Drum Point
6 front lower range	**18** Hooper Island
7 front upper range	**19** Point No Point
8 rear upper range	**20** Solomons Lump
9 Seven Foot Knoll	**21** Point Lookout
10 Baltimore	**22** Piney Point
11 Sandy Point Shoal	**23** Fort Washington

VIRGINIA LIGHTS	
24 Jones Point	**30** Newport News
25 Smith Point	Middle Ground
26 Wolf Trap	**31** Cape Henry - new
27 New Point Comfort	**32** Cape Henry - old
28 Thimble Shoal	**33** Cape Charles
29 Old Point Comfort	**34** Chesapeake

Map by: Michele Allen Danoff

Concord Point

On August 8, 1826, a 484-square-foot tract of land was deeded to the U.S. Government by the Commissioners of the Town of Havre de Grace for the establishment of a light station at Concord Point. The Concord lighthouse (the name is a corruption of Conquered Point, in turn, a variation of the original name, Point of Conquest), commissioned on May 21, 1827, was designed to protect vessels from dangerous shoals and currents at the mouth of the Susquehanna River.

The lighthouse was built by John Donahoo, the most prominent contractor in early Chesapeake Bay lighthouse construction (and, in the years between 1819-1839, a man who served several terms as a town commissioner of Havre de Grace).

The stone masonry walls of the lighthouse, three feet, 11 inches thick at the base with an interior diameter of 11 feet, were constructed of Port Deposit granite and, unlike Donahoo's first attempt at lighthouse construction at Thomas Point (a lighthouse which had to be rebuilt in 1838), the Concord Point light tower has withstood the test of time. In fact, when the light was decommissioned by the U.S. Coast Guard in 1975, Concord Point light had achieved the distinction of being the oldest lighthouse in continuous use in the State of Maryland.

Another man who became town commissioner of Havre de Grace, John O'Neill, also figured prominently in the history of the light station. Born in Ireland in 1768, O'Neill immigrated to the United States when he was 18 years old and chose Havre de Grace as his home. On May 3, 1813, as a fleet of British ships under the command of Admiral Sir George Cockburn began to bombard Havre de Grace, O'Neill—then a local militia lieutenant—found himself in charge of a group of about 50 men at a small breastwork of three cannon called the Potato Battery. When the British began to fire on the town, O'Neill's men (many of them apparently too old to serve in the regular army) fled inland leaving him alone with the cannon. Undaunted, he served one cannon by himself. "The grape shot flew thick about me," he later recalled.

This photograph, taken in the late 19th century after a second story had been added to the keeper's dwelling, shows the configuration of the point before development to the south of Fayette Street took place. Photo, Chesapeake Bay Maritime Museum.

Starke Jett

"I loaded the gun myself without anyone to serve the vent, which, you know is very dangerous, and [when] I fired her...she recoiled and ran over my thigh."

"I retreated down to town," he continued, "and joined Mr. Barnes of the nail manufactory with a musket and fired on the barges while we had ammunition, and then retreated to the common, where I kept waving my hat to the militia, who had run away, to come to our assistance."

O'Neill was captured and taken aboard the Maidstone frigate and sentenced to be hanged. When his 15-year-old daughter, Matilda, learned of his capture and impending doom, she rowed out to the Maidstone in a small skiff to intervene on his behalf, producing her father's commission papers to prove that he was not a civilian. Impressed by the young woman's bravery, Admiral Cockburn released O'Neill and gave Matilda his gold-mounted, tortoise-shell snuff box (now in possession of the Maryland Historical Society).

O'Neill became the town hero and when the Concord Point light was commissioned (at a time when the selection of keepers was still clearly a political appointment) there was no question that O'Neill should receive the honor of being named as keeper, a position which he retained until he died in January, 1838. The honor was then extended to his descendants, several of whom kept the light in the years before 1920 when it was automated. The O'Neill keepers include John O'Neill, Jr., who served from 1838, after the death of his father, until 1841; a grandson, John O'Neill, 1860-1863; Esther O'Neill, 1863-1870, wife of John O'Neill, Jr.; Henry O'Neill, 1881-1919, also a grandson of John O'Neill; and Harry O'Neill, 1919-1920, great-grandson of John O'Neill. These were not, however, the only keepers of the Concord Point light.

According to the annual reports of the Light-House Board, Donahoo's sturdy granite tower has required surprisingly little in the way of major repair over the years. In 1855, the old reflecting apparatus (nine constant-level lamps and nine 16-inch reflectors) was replaced with a steamer's lens and this lens, in turn, was replaced with a sixth-order Fresnel lens in 1869. In 1884, an additional story was added to the keeper's quarters and, finally, the sixth-order lens was replaced by one of the fifth-order in 1891.

In 1991 the Maryland Historical Trust reported that, except for inadequate ventilation in the lantern, the lighthouse remains in good condition. The exterior surface of the truncated conical tower has been coated with Roman cement and the brick masonry pavers of the ground floor remain solid, though they have heaved slightly in places. The spiral stairway to the lantern is constructed of triangular granite treads that lead to a quarter-circle stone landing where an iron ship's ladder, angling gently across the stone stairwell, provides a dizzying climb to the unusual nine-sided lantern and lantern deck. The lantern and lantern deck floor are also of radially cut solid stone joined together with five-inch-long flat iron keys. The iron mullions which hold the lantern's storm panels are of an uncommon fin-shape.

In 1920 the station was electrified. At that time, a portion of the lighthouse reservation, including the keeper's dwelling, was sold for $4,000. For many years thereafter, the former keeper's quarters were operated as an inn. Meanwhile, the property immediately surrounding the lighthouse was neglected. In 1975, when, for reasons of economy, the light station was decommissioned by the Coast Guard, the beautiful and irreplaceable Fresnel lens disappeared. Alarmed at the loss of this historical treasure, local citizens banded together to ensure the protection and restoration of the lighthouse and, in 1979, formed a non-profit organization, The Friends of Concord Point Lighthouse.

Today the old tower has been restored and is open to the public from May through October. The modest tree-lined park surrounding the lighthouse at the end of Lafayette Street is beautifully maintained and the lighthouse receives thousands of visitors annually. A small floating pier also provides pleasure boat access to the park grounds.

In recent years, the old keeper's quarters have once again been purchased and are being restored by The Friends of Concord Point Lighthouse. In 1990, The Friends of Concord Point Lighthouse commissioned an architectural and historic study of the keeper's dwelling, a first step towards restoration of the keeper's quarters.* The house, which has been modified many times in the past 170 years, is separated from the lighthouse tower by over 200 feet—an unusual distance when one considers that the keeper needed to climb the tower several times during the night. Concord Street, however, which now separates the house and lighthouse tower, had not yet been extended to the south and thus, although the dwelling does sit on a separate (and separately purchased) parcel of land, the keeper originally enjoyed an unobstructed view of the tower and the confluence of the Susquehanna River and the Chesapeake Bay beyond. At the time the house was built, the land surrounding the lighthouse complex was open and grassy and there were few trees of significant size. (Town records actually show that John O'Neill hired a cart and horses to fill in a swampy area behind the keeper's house.) Most of the original parcel has now been sold and subdivided—or has been covered in asphalt for parking space—and the original dwelling, modified by a variety of additions (including a second story) and innumerable partitions, has likewise been hidden under stucco, scrolled to look like stone.

The 1827 building contract called for a solid but modest house "of stone or hard brick" (Donahoo used Port Deposit granite), 34 feet by 20 feet, with a fireplace and a closet in each room, large double-hung windows (eight panes over eight panes of glass), and a shingled roof. A kitchen was to be attached to the house and was to contain "a chimney with a fireplace, and sizable oven with an iron door, iron crane, trammel and hooks in the fireplace, and on one side of the chimney a sink, with a spout leading through the wall." None of the original kitchen now survives.

When the keeper's quarters and outbuildings are complete, the site will afford visitors the opportunity to see how lighthouse keepers and their families lived during the early part of the 19th century. Although no longer an active navigational aid, The Friends of Concord Point Lighthouse still proudly display the beacon in a fifth-order Fresnel lens—believed by some to be, in fact, the original lens—on loan from the U.S. Coast Guard and the Chesapeake Bay Maritime Museum.

---

* The report was prepared by the Clio Group, Inc., and John M. Adams, Architect. The study was funded by The Friends of Concord Point Lighthouse and The Maryland Historical Trust.

Fishing Battery

The construction of a lighthouse on the small man-made island, variously known as Fishing Battery, Edmondson Island, Shad Battery, and Donahoo's Battery was authorized by an Act of Congress in 1851. Situated two and one-half miles below the mouth of the Susquehanna River, it is believed that the island was built as a landing place where the large fishing nets then used on the Susquehanna Flats could be wound in and the fish unloaded on a platform before being taken to market. Here, too, paddle-boats that could not enter Havre de Grace, would pick up the fishermen's catch and head back to Baltimore. (By the end of the 19th century, the island boasted a large government-run fish hatchery, fish-processing enterprises, and a steamboat landing.)

Congress made an appropriation of $5,000 for erection of the station, and John Donahoo—by this time an old hand at lighthouse construction on the bay—was awarded the contract to build the 32-foot lighthouse dwelling with a rooftop lantern. The station was completed and the light commissioned in 1853. (Fishing Battery is the last lighthouse built by Donahoo on the bay.)

Many lighthouse buffs and historians have observed that a curious deal surrounds the government's acquisition of the Fishing Battery property. For one thing, the government purchased the land twice, once from a Mr. Otho Scott—who was paid $600 for the 45-by-45-foot tract of land—and once again, two weeks later, from Donahoo himself, who sold the same parcel of land to the government for $10. There seems to be no question that at one time Donahoo did own the land, but apparently he had lost title to it about 10 years before the date of the aforementioned sale. Eventually, the matter was resolved when the purchase from Otho Scott was given the official stamp of approval by the U.S. attorney general. Given Donahoo's business acumen and his long association with the Department of Treasury as a lighthouse contractor, it seems highly unlikely that he would have sold the tract for only $10 if indeed he thought he still owned the land.

Fishing Battery light, before 1921. Additional buildings, most of them constructed by the Bureau of Fisheries after leasing the island in the 1880's, included a store house, a mess shed, an icehouse, coal bins and a boiler, a mechanic's cottage and another residence. Photo, Chesapeake Bay Maritime Museum.

Starke Jett

A few years after the Fishing Battery lighthouse was completed, the illuminating apparatus was replaced with a sixth-order Fresnel lens. In 1864, the lantern was also replaced—the Board noting that the lantern at Fishing Battery was one of several on the bay "of an old an exceedingly defective character," and that "the interests of commerce demand that steps be taken to remedy the evil." Once again, in 1867, Fishing Battery, Pooles Island, Turkey Point, and Concord Light all received "new and improved" lanterns. Finally, in 1899 a "new-model" fifth-order lens was installed.

From 1880 to 1891, the island was leased to the United States Bureau of Fisheries who, according to the Light-House Board, made "extensive improvements" to the lighthouse property by "raising the grade of the island."

"To conform to the new grade and for sanitary reasons," the Board reported in 1887, "it was found necessary to remove the lower floor of the light-house, fill the inclosure with clean soil and lay a concrete floor." As was the case at Concord Point light, the walls were elevated and the dwelling enlarged, apparently creating some additional living space for the keeper and his family; it was replastered, reroofed and a new porch was built. But at Fishing Battery the lower level was redesigned to be used as a boathouse and storage room; the second-level main floor of the dwelling afforded the keeper and his family their only living quarters—essentially no more than a combination kitchen and sitting room plus two bedrooms.

Meanwhile, the Bureau of Fisheries continued to use the island as a fish hatchery and eventually purchased the island for $15,000. The caption of an 1887 drawing of the lighthouse reservation takes inventory of some of the Bureau's improvements: a large fish basin, a hatchery and a gated "carp pond" (actually used for shad fingerlings), a storehouse, a mess shed, an icehouse, coal bins and a boiler, a water tower, a boat basin, a mechanic's cottage and another residence—all in addition to the lighthouse proper.

In 1921 the light was changed to acetylene gas and placed on a 38-foot steel tower which stands today next to the old lighthouse. The station was automated in 1939—at the time that the U.S. Coast Guard took over all navigational aids—but the light, now solar-powered, remains active.

On June 23, 1942, Executive Order 9185 transferred "all of Shad Battery, or Edmondson Island, to the Department of the Interior as a refuge and breeding ground for migratory birds and other wildlife subject to no interference with the use of the small area for lighthouse purposes." The reservation was known as the Susquehanna Wildlife Refuge but, eventually, the island fell under the jurisdiction of the Blackwater Wildlife Refuge which, in addition to their large sanctuary in Dorchester County farther to the south, managed about 30,000 acres in the Susquehanna Flats.

In more recent years, the lamentable loss of habitat for migratory waterfowl on the upper bay and the rapid erosion of the island have been important considerations in a community effort, led by the Havre de Grace Maritime Museum and the Battery Island Preservation Society, to reclaim the island and to incorporate it into a regional complex of museums and historic landmarks detailing the history and ecology of the upper bay.

Working closely with the Havre de Grace Maritime Museum, the Battery Island Preservation Society, formed in 1990, has sought access to the scant remains of the island with plans to restore the lighthouse dwelling in order to make the island into a public recreation facility featuring a bed and breakfast inn. With help from Congress, a 99-year lease agreement between the Department of Interior, the Battery Island Preservation Society, the U.S. Coast Guard, the Maryland Department of Natural Resources, the Blackwater Wildlife Refuge and other agencies with some rights in the use of the island and its environs, was verbally worked out. But, in the end, when an attempt was made to spell out the agreement in writing, the lease was not signed. First of all, there was apparently a purely technical question of liability during the actual transfer of the property—essentially a problem of phrasing. Secondly, and perhaps more importantly, there was a fear on the part of some that a precedent might be established with regard to the future of other reserved lands—even though the land in question is fast disappearing and even though, in this particular instance, all the agencies concerned with wildlife preservation apparently support the project.

Meanwhile, the old lighthouse is being subjected to vandalism of an increasingly destructive nature. Since 1992, the interior stair treads (from the ground floor all the way to the lantern), shutters, window sashes, sills, moldings and other timbers have been ripped out and used for bonfires and campfires by ribald overnight visitors to the island. According to one observer, each year brings more weekend vacationers in high-speed pleasure craft to the island. In the summer of 1994, a metal sign identifying the building as an historic landmark and restoration project disappeared the same weekend that it was installed—along with new protective plywood coverings for the windows and doors.

Nevertheless, local architects, engineers and other citizens have donated their time to complete feasibility studies and to draw up plans for the restoration. First of all, they want to stabilize the island, taking it back to its original acreage—over seven acres of riparian rights are established. The society has obtained engineering estimates for the reconstruction of the stone bulkheads which formerly surrounded the island and the reports are promising: most of the bulkheading is still there and only needs to be moved back into place. Reconstruction of the boat turnaround and the lighthouse cistern is also feasible. There are detailed plans to restore the lighthouse (which is still structurally sound), including its cast-iron lantern, and the keeper's boathouse on the ground level. Finally, local rumor has it that the whereabouts of the original Fresnel lens is known and that it will be anonymously returned when the lighthouse is restored. In addition, there are plans to rebuild some of the other outbuildings—important to the region's economic activities in the late 19th century—that have long since disappeared. When completed, these will be used as part of the recreational facility, but the process of working through the bureaucratic red tape is painfully slow.

Turkey Point

On March 3, 1831, Congress appropriated $5,000 for construction of a lighthouse on a four-acre plot at Turkey Point, a bluff that separates the Elk and Northeast rivers at the head of the Chesapeake Bay. In fact, the yellow-brown cliffs have long been a well-known landmark to mariners of the bay; Captain John Smith, for example, took note of the high bluff on his first excursion into the Chesapeake in the early 1600's.

The lighthouse tower and compact keeper's dwelling were built by John Donahoo for $4,355 and the light was commissioned in 1833. Although the height of the tower is only 35 feet (30 feet from its base to the center of the

The old fog-bell tower and lookout at Turkey Point. The fog bell was attached to the outside of the tower and a 30-foot well was dug to accommodate the weights of the winding mechanism. Photo (c. 1930), U.S. Coast Guard.

lantern), the 100-foot precipice on which it stands greatly increases the height of the light, making it—at 129 feet above mean high water—one of the highest lights on the Chesapeake Bay.

Structurally, the Turkey Point light is very similar to other lighthouse towers built by Donahoo. In fact, Donahoo used the very same plans for the Havre de Grace and Turkey Point lights, though there are some variations in building materials used; for example, the spiral stairway leading to the lantern at Concord Point light is made of stone while the stair treads at Turkey Point were built of cast-iron.

Turkey Point light is a brick masonry tower forming the frustum of a cone topped with a narrow widow's walk that is cantilevered a few inches from the outer rim of the tower. The nine-sided lantern has rectangular storm panels and a pyramidal iron roof topped with a ventilator ball. The lantern gallery is surrounded by narrow cast-iron balusters and three rows of circular railings. Originally painted red and showing a fixed white light, the lantern was changed to black sometime before the latter part of the 19th century and its signal was changed to flashing white when the light was fully automated in 1947.

In the 1850's, one of the first undertakings of the newly organized Light-

Starke Jett

Keeper Fannie Salter and her son feed the turkeys that she kept on the property. Salter successfully petitioned President Coolidge to remain as keeper of Turkey Point after the sudden death of her husband. She remained as keeper until her retirement in 1947. Photo, The National Archives.

Light station established:
1833

**Construction of
present structure:**
1833

Location:
On the bluff point separating
the mouths of the Elk and
Northeast Rivers, at the head of
the Chesapeake Bay, Maryland.

Position:
39 27 00
76 00 31

Characteristic of light:
Flashing white; red sector
from 080 to 120 degrees,
covering the entrance to the
Susquehanna River.

**Height of light, above
mean high water:**
129 feet; tower is 35 feet.

Range:
White, 8 miles; red, 6 miles.

Description of station:
White masonry tower with
black lantern; keepers dwelling
and fog-bell tower have been
torn down.

House Board was to see to the installation of Fresnel lenses in all U. S. light-houses. According to the annual reports of the Light-House Board, the first Fresnel lens was placed in the tower at Turkey Point in 1856; eight years later, in 1864, the lantern was completely refitted and, then, in 1868, a Franklin lamp was substituted for the old constant-level lamp. The Light-House Board found the light station in good condition in 1869.

During the 1880's a number of improvements were made to the dwelling and outbuildings and a fog bell was added to the station. "The stable was rebuilt," the Board noted in its 1885 annual report, "and a new platform and windlass were made for the well..." Because of the height of the bluff, and therefore the distance of the light station from the water, the placement of the fog bell posed some problems if it was to be heard by passing ships, and a well was excavated for the weights of the winding mechanisms. Olga Salter Crouch (daughter of the station's last lightkeeper) remembers that the fog-bell house stood approximately 100 feet from the tower.

> *The fog bell was suspended on the outside of the building and rung by a Gamewell Fire Alarm Machine...that worked like a large grandfather clock. It had a pendulum and was powered by heavy weights on a cable that ran down a 30-foot-deep well. The bell sounded every fifteen seconds and the weights had to be rewound every two hours and forty-five minutes. A rope was attached to the bell's clapper and was used to salute boats—and, also, to ring the bell manually when the Gamewell machine failed.*

In 1889, the Light-House Board reported: "The dwelling was raised one story, by which four habitable rooms were secured, and a new front porch was built." Turkey Point now offered a fine, if somewhat remote, home to its keepers and their families.

Between 1833, when the light was first commissioned, and 1939—when the Coast Guard took over the lighthouse service—Turkey Point had a number of single women keepers, and none of them was written about more frequently than Fannie Salter.*

Although by the time of her husband's death in 1925, the Civil Service Commission had specifically ruled against the hiring of women light-keepers, Salter fought for her job and was finally elevated from assistant keeper to keeper by President Calvin Coolidge.

Like many other civilian keepers, Fannie Salter chose to remain at her isolated post when the lighthouse service was placed under direction of the U.S. Coast Guard. When she retired in 1947, she was admiringly—and a bit humorously—touted in the New York Mirror as "the last of the lady light-house keepers." In fact, her retirement brought a long tradition of employment for women to an end—a tradition that, in fact, seemed much more un-usual in the mid 20th-century than it had 100 years earlier when husband and wife often shared equally in the economic enterprises of the family.

* Other women keepers with long tenure at Turkey Point include Elizabeth Lusby (wife of Turkey Point's first keeper, Robert Lusby), who served as main keeper from May 1844 to March 1862; Rebecca Crouch, who was officially appointed in October 1873, two months after her husband died (though she had been at the light station for eight years already) until her death in July 1895; and Georgiana Brumfield, daughter of a former keeper at Turkey Point, who remained at the post until 1923.

Until the light was electrified in 1942, Salter toted a copper kettle filled with kerosene up the 31 steps of the spiral stairway and the narrow rungs of the iron ship's ladder from the top of the tower into lantern, every night, four times a night. Likewise, until that same year, when the Coast Guard also installed an electric foghorn at the light station, Salter wound the machinery that rang the enormous fog bell every two-and-three-quarter hours when foggy or stormy weather reduced or obscured the light's visibility. Remarkably, wooden steps led down the face of the bluff and were regularly used by the keeper when supply boats brought necessary provisions to the light (these deliveries were always made by boat). A winch was used to haul the stores up to the light.

When Salter retired in 1947 and the light was fully automated, a light sensor was installed to turn the light on during cloudy weather and use of an automatic sensing device was also introduced to activate the foghorn during periods of low visibility.

In spite of its remote location within Elk Neck State Park (one must walk a mile from the nearest parking lot to see the light), vandalism has taken its toll on the lighthouse tower in the years since the last Coast Guard keeper was removed. Regrettably, the damage inflicted on the light station by vandals has been countered with protective measures which have further marred the integrity of the lighthouse station. First of all, a large section of the interior spiral stairway was removed when the original door was broken down and the exquisite Fresnel lens stolen from the lantern. The original wooden door was replaced with a solid steel door without ventilation panels, and, at the same time, unventilated acrylic panes were also used to glaze the windows.

The keeper's house was also irreparably damaged by vandalism and neglect. Finally, in 1972, the Maryland State Forest and Park Service tore it down. First of all, they had no funds to maintain or repair the dwelling and, second, as both park rangers and private citizens of the nearby town of Northeast, Maryland are quick to point out, the keeper's house was in such poor repair that it had become a danger to visitors to the park.

On a wistful note, there is now talk among some local folk of building a facsimile of the old keeper's dwelling. The project has some enthusiastic supporters and plans have been drawn up, though, clearly, there are many obstacles to overcome in the realization of such a scheme. First of all, the Coast Guard maintains an active light at Turkey Point and its jurisdiction with regard to the station is paramount. Second, the Maryland Historical Trust has very precise standards for the reconstruction of historical landmarks; a true facsimile dwelling would be expensive both to build and to maintain. Third, compliance with public health regulations would necessitate considerable expense—there was never a sewer system of any kind at the point. Electricity would have to be brought back out—there is no source now. Last but not least, someone would need to live on the property to ensure that vandalism did not once again destroy the house. Nevertheless, there is support for the idea and the Maryland Department of Natural Resources has expressed an interest in leasing the property for development as an historical site. Presently the rangers at Elk Neck State Park estimate that the lighthouse tower is visited by 50,000-60,000 people annually.

Pooles Island

Named by Captain John Smith for one of his crew members, Nathaniel Powell, on his 1608 excursion into the Chesapeake Bay (and in its almost 400-year history variously known as Powell's Island, Pool's Island and Poole's Island—with or without the apostrophe), Pooles Island is now a part of the Aberdeen Proving Ground and off-limits to the public because of unexploded ordnance in the vicinity.* The Pooles Island light—one of the oldest lights on the Chesapeake Bay—is conspicuously untended, the keeper's dwelling has long since been torn down, and the landscape surrounding the lighthouse has a wild beauty and, at least along the beach, a desolate aspect. Today it is difficult to envision the small but prosperous agricultural community that, in the late 19th and early 20th centuries, supplied Baltimoreans with choice peaches from early July through mid-October.

In 1849—at a time when prizefighting was outlawed in Maryland—Pooles Island became the site of a famous prizefight. Apparently, then-governor Philip Thomas forbade steamboat captains to take spectators to the island and called out troops to prevent the match from taking place, but the governor's boat went aground and the spectators arrived on Pooles Island on oystermen's skipjacks. The story goes that people waved gaily at the troops, still hard aground, as they sailed back to Baltimore after the fight.

In 1917, when the U.S. Army acquired the island, the keeper was removed though the light remained active. This 1928 photo shows the comfortable keeper's dwelling (which was torn down about ten years later). Photo, U.S. Coast Guard.

The long, narrow island of approximately 280 acres was purchased by Peregrine Wethered in 1808. Relying heavily on slave labor, Wethered ran the island as a highly successful wheat farm. Though it was plundered by the British in the War of 1812, the island rebounded with crops that in the late 19th century were remembered as "the wonder and admiration of the farmers all along the bay." Both the character of the soil (described as a rich black loam varying in depth from 18 inches to eight feet) and much of the vegetation on Pooles Island were thought to be quite different from that of nearby Harford and Kent counties. Early settlers, for example, commented that they found no chestnuts or pines on Pooles Island though they were abundant on the nearby mainland.

Congressional authorization for construction of the lighthouse was made in May of 1824 and the lighthouse, constructed by John Donahoo, was com-

*Although the origin of the island's name is not disputed, the evolution of the name also appears to be related to the presence of several spring-fed fresh-water pools on the island. In the 19th and early 20th centuries Pooles Island was apparently viewed as a rather exotic place. "Numerous wells of clear sparkling water are scattered about the island," an article in *The Baltimore Sun* proclaimed at the turn of the century. "The water also differs from that usually found along the bay, being soft instead of hard, resembling greatly that found on the high lands in the western counties."

Starke Jett

15

Light station established:
1825

Construction of present structure:
1825

Location:
On Pooles Island, off the mouth of the Gunpowder River, Maryland.

Position:
39 17 26
76 16 00

Characteristic of light:
Inactive.

Height of light, above mean high water:
Light was formerly shown at 38 feet.

Description of station:
Masonry tower in poor repair. Detached dwelling and fog-bell tower have been torn down.

pleted in 1825 at a cost of $5,000 on a six-acre parcel of land purchased from Peregrine Wethered for $500. Along with the old Cape Henry light, commissioned in 1791, and the Old and New Point Comfort lights, commissioned in 1804, the Pooles Island tower is one of the oldest original lighthouse structures still standing on the bay—and the oldest original lighthouse still standing in Maryland.

In 1872, 7,000 peach trees were set out by George Merrett when he purchased the island from Peregrine Wethered's son, John. This was the beginning of the island's reputation as an orchard. Ten years later, the island was purchased by Charles C. Homer, president of the Second National Bank of Baltimore, and John J. Masheter, a prosperous farmer from Ohio. Returning from a fishing trip on the bay, Masheter enthusiastically informed Homer that he "had found a piece of Iowa soil in Maryland" and that he yearned to buy it. Shortly thereafter, Homer and Masheter did purchase the island and they expanded the peach orchards. Among the many varieties of peaches grown in a season that lasted from midsummer until late fall was one of their own development—*Pool's Island Best*. Contemporary newspaper accounts stated that many of the peach trees attained a size almost unknown to fruit growers—with trunks between 10 and 18 inches in diameter. "[The soil] is so rich," an article about the island gushed in the late years of the 19th century, "that the abundant crops are produced today without the aid of fertilizers, none but the manure made on the place ever having been used on it in its 100 years of cultivation."

The lighthouse is a conical tower 40 feet and 6 inches in overall height (the tower is 28 feet tall and the lantern is 12 feet 6 inches) and constructed of randomly laid, rough-cut granite blocks with irregularly sized mortar joints. The granite was quarried in Port Deposit. Beneath the cement foundation and floor of the tower, wooden pilings support and help to distribute the weight of the stone structure which tapers from an 18-foot diameter at its base to a nine-foot diameter at the top of the tower. The spiral steps which wind around the interior wall to the landing at the top of the tower are solid cut granite. Both the lantern cupola and lantern deck, which is cantilevered a few inches beyond the rim of the tower, are cast iron. The tower was stuccoed and whitewashed, inside and out.

In 1828, Congress appropriated another $2,800 for construction of a fog-bell tower. In 1857, shortly after the establishment of the Light-House Board, the reflecting apparatus was replaced with a fourth-order Fresnel lens.

According to the reports of the Light-House Board, the station was severely damaged by a storm in June of 1881. The following year, the small keeper's dwelling was enlarged. "The brick-work was built up on the masonry, another story, of three rooms, was added to the dwelling, and a new tin roof was then put on; the fencing was repaired and the lantern and fog-bell tower were painted. The station is now in good condition," the Board concluded.

One surmises from the annual reports that the location of the lighthouse afforded a comfortable and pleasant home for its keepers and their families. New fencing and outbuildings, plank (and later brick) walkways around the keeper's grounds and between the dwelling and two towers, were added to

16

the station. "A new front porch, cow-stable, and poultry-house were built and various repairs were made," the Board noted in 1887. In 1890, "486 feet of picket fence and 34 feet of post-and-rail fence were built." Two years later, a boat house was added and "a windlass was provided for hauling up boats." Improvements were continued at the light station until the island was acquired by the U.S. Army in 1917 to become part of the Aberdeen Proving Ground and arrangements were made to remove the keeper and automate the light. In 1939, the property was turned over to the War Department, "in good condition," and, shortly thereafter, the light was deactivated and the lens was removed. The attractive house with its wide front porch was demolished.

On the one hand, because of its inaccessibility as part of a military reservation and the dangers of live artillery in the immediate vicinity of the tower, Pooles Island light faces a unique set of problems with regard to its preservation as an historic landmark. The exterior of the 170-year-old tower is in poor repair. There is practically no stucco or paint left on the masonry and the surface appears to be crumbling in places. Ivy grows up one side of the tower. The cast-iron lantern and gallery, which is cantilevered from the top deck of the tower, are also in need of paint. The lantern roof, the iron mullions which frame the storm panels, and the cast-iron balustrade appear to be in sound condition but in need of paint. Essentially, the light has been abandoned for over 50 years. The pedestal which once supported the light has been removed from the lantern and sits amid the sand and grass close to the tower. Nearby a faintly etched stone marks the grave of Elijah Williams and honors the memory of his brother James, two mariners who were lost in a snowstorm in February of 1855 (James' body was never recovered).

Eventually, the U.S. Army would like to restore the lighthouse property as a gift to the public, but security, both from the point of view of public safety, and with regard to securing the lighthouse from vandals if the site is developed, poses difficulties requiring expensive solutions. In addition, the island's shoreline is eroding and needs to be riprapped or bulkheaded to ensure that the tower remains on dry land. (The military observation post is now practically in the water.) In 1994, the Army petitioned to have the light placed on the National Historic Register.

On the other hand, the unwitting legacy of the army's 60-year bombardment of the island has kept it from developers and afforded a much-needed sanctuary for wildlife on the bay (and one can only hope that this unintended refuge will remain undisturbed). Secondary growth now covers much of the island (there are practically no original hardwoods). Ivy and grapevines twist around rows of long-dead peach trees; herds of deer, who some believe crossed to the island from the Edgewood area during a bad freeze in 1978, now abound on the isolated retreat. There are nesting eagles, a blue-heron rookery and wintering geese. Right next door to the lighthouse, an osprey pair have found that a galvanized steel tower with a rickety wooden platform—still sometimes used by the military to observe shelling rounds and to keep an eye out for boats that might come too close to the island—now offers a hospitable nesting site with an unobstructed view of the bay.

Craighill Channel, Lower Range

There are two sets of range lights named after William Price Craighill (1833-1909), a long-time member of the Light-House Board who supervised the engineering surveys of the channel, and this can be a source of confusion for the novice lighthouse buff or for someone just becoming familiar with the lights of the Chesapeake Bay.* There is a lower range, commissioned in 1873, and an upper range, commissioned in 1886, often called the Cutoff Channel. Each range contains a front light and a rear light. The lower Craighill range is the older of the two ranges and consists of one of the smallest caisson structures and one of the tallest towers on the bay.

The Craighill Channel leads from the Chesapeake Bay into the Brewerton Channel of the Patapsco River, intersecting it at a point (approximately one mile northeast of Seven Foot Knoll) that saves large vessels five miles on their approach to Baltimore from the lower bay. (Although the original Brewerton Channel lighthouses—Hawkins Point and Leading Point—are now gone, the range itself is still marked by two lights, a small beacon and a skeleton tower, that flash green 24 hours a day.)

The first estimate for construction of the Craighill lights was submitted in 1870. At that time the Craighill Channel was new and the estimate that the Board submitted was "for two screw-pile lights to serve as a range by day and by night."

All lighthouse enthusiasts regret destruction of the unusual Victorian dwelling that afforded quarters to the keeper of the rear light of the Craighill Channel Lower Range. The original piers of Port Deposit granite are visible. Photo, The Mariners' Museum, Newport News.

> *The channel is now 200 feet wide, with a depth at mean low tide of 21 feet. It will be completed during the current fiscal year at a probable width varying from 300 to 500 feet, and it is urged that it is of the utmost importance, in order that it may be safely used day and night, that these two light-houses be authorized and built at the earliest practicable moment.*

In addition, the Board pointed out that the sooner "propeller steamers" could begin to use the channel, the better, for, "more than anything else" they would serve "to keep it open and possibly improve it, thereby relieving the Government from an annual expense for dredging."

The following year, the Board continued to push enthusiastically for construction of the range lights, elaborating at length on the channel's importance and noting repeatedly that "the urgency of making it available at night for the large commerce of the city of Baltimore is manifest."

Congress had already appropriated $50,000 to widen the Craighill Channel to 500 feet and deepen it to 22 feet, mean low tide, and had spent a considerable sum for improvements to the Brewerton Channel, which, the Board reluctantly admitted, "is acknowledged to be of great benefit to navigation"—especially, the report added, since the Brewerton Channel with its range lights, unlike the new Craighill Channel, could be followed at night.

* Craighill distinguished himself as a student and teacher at West Point, as an Army engineer and a brevet colonel during the Civil War, and, in 1895, years after both sets of range lights had been completed, Craighill became chief of the Army Corps of Engineers.

Starke Jett

REAR LIGHT

Light station established:
1873

Location:
On shoal, near the southerly end of Hart Island, 2 1/2 miles in rear of preceding (4800 yards, 000 degrees from front light), on the direct prolongation of axis of Craighill Channel, Maryland.

Position:
39 13 (41)
76 23 (37)

Characteristic of Light:
Fixed white.

Height of light, above mean high water:
105 feet.

Distance visible, in nautical miles:
16

Description of Station:
Open frame pyramid of four sides; lower portion, white; upper part, brown.

But the new Craighill Channel, the Board pleaded, would allow vessels to avoid the large accumulations of ice in the lower part of the Brewerton Channel and once completed it would tend to maintain itself:

> *It is an established fact that the current produced by the outflow of water from the river and bay tends to deepen the channel by washing out the material on the bottom, and there is no doubt but that this channel, once improved to a depth of twenty-two and width of five hundred feet, will always maintain at least those dimensions.*

Finally, the Board noted that the establishment of the Craighill Channel lights would "render the use of those at North Point unnecessary, and they can be discontinued." The Board asked for an appropriation of $45,000.

In the end, Congress complied with the request and plans were drawn up for the rear and front range lights though, by now, there was enough disenchantment with screwpile lighthouses to warrant consideration of other types of structures. Referring to the front light, the Board was clearly worried about moving ice.

> *During the winter of 1872-73...the ice formed so heavily in the Chesapeake Bay, in the vicinity of the proposed site of this light-house that it was deemed advisable to change the plan and build a more solid structure that could, beyond all doubt, safely withstand the heavy ice-floes by which it will be assailed.*

Construction of both lighthouses proved difficult and expensive, and both had to be outfitted with temporary lights while additional appropriations for their completion were sought. First of all, the severe winter of 1872-73 caused delays in locating the range line in the long and narrow channel. Work on the foundation of the rear light did not begin until the following April at which time it was discovered that the substratum of the site posed some unusual challenges.

> *A careful examination showed that the soil on top was firm, hard sand, to a depth of two feet. Below this was a thin layer of sand and mud, mixed with stones, then soft mud to a depth of fifteen feet.*

It was decided to construct a cofferdam, 60 feet by 60 feet, using two rows of sheet piling, 18 inches apart and filled with "clay pudding," to enclose the entire area.

> *The sheet piling was put down with rapidity and satisfactorily by the water-jet process. The dam was then pumped out, and the foundation piles (after some delay owing to the breaking of the dam on two occasions during heavy gales) were driven and cut off.*

In June, the framework was finished and the nine supporting piers, built of Port Deposit granite, were completed in August, but the Board needed an additional $10,000 to complete the lighthouse. "The cost of this structure was necessarily increased by the difficulties encountered in getting a secure foundation," the Board acknowledged, "and the appropriation that was made for the two range-lights (front and rear) will not be sufficient to complete them."

The rear lighthouse was an unusual structure, unique on the bay: an open framework forming the frustum of a four-sided pyramid with corner columns of cast iron resting on cast-iron disks anchored to the masonry of the piers. A handsome two-story keeper's house with dormer windows was built within the base of the pyramid. From the roof of this dwelling, a stairway enclosed by a rectangular shaft led to the watch area and the lantern—both with unusual cantilevered decks—whose focal plane is 105 feet above mean high tide. Unfortunately, when the light was automated in the 1930's, the keeper's dwelling was torn down.

Likewise, construction of the front light involved a change of plans and additional money. As mentioned, the screwpile structure was scrapped in favor of "a tubular foundation of cast iron," but, once again, the character of the soil substratum posed difficulties.

> [F]or a depth of 22 feet the soil is the softest kind of mud, so soft, in fact, that an ordinary pile, stood on end, would penetrate 20 feet under the action of its own weight. Below this, alternate thin layers of sand, mixtures of sand, mud, and shell were found to a depth of 20 feet more, with no signs of a solid foundation within 60 feet of the water's surface.

The engineers decided to drive a cluster of piles into the muddy shoal and cut them off 27 feet below the surface of the water. The caisson would then be lowered into place on top of this foundation. "The change in the character of this structure from what was first intended," the Board stated in its report, "will add considerably to its cost, and an additional appropriation of $25,000 is therefore asked for."

The first attempt to position the caisson in October 1873 was unsuccessful and it had to be refloated and repositioned. To prevent scour, 5,000 tons of riprap stone were placed around the base.

When the Board submitted its annual report the following year, both lights were nearing completion and had been outfitted with temporary beacons—and, as was apparently customary, the lighthouse keepers had moved to their stations before their housing was readied. The keepers of the rear light were given accommodations in the workmen's quarters, while the front-light keepers were housed in a temporary frame house, also used to support a fourth-order lantern. The front-light caisson was surrounded by 5,000 tons of broken stone, still visible at the surface of the water at low tide.

In 1875, both structures were finally finished and, with another 675 cubic yards of riprap stone deposited around the front-light caisson, the Board noted with satisfaction that "[t]he heavy ice of the past winter did no damage to this station, though the locality is one of great exposure."

Interestingly, the front-light caisson has always had two lights—one in the lantern and one mounted on the side of the circular dwelling—and has thus

The keepers of the front light of the Craighill Channel Lower Range pose with a party of rescuers on the frozen waters of the Chesapeake Bay. Photo (n.d.), Chesapeake Bay Maritime Museum.

served both as a bay lighthouse and as a range light. The focal plane of the lighthouse lantern is 39 feet; the focal point of the range light is 22 feet and it can be seen housed in an iron-plate enclosure that protrudes from the first level of the circular cast-iron dwelling. The fixed white range lights are kept burning 24 hours a day, whereas the lantern is lit from sundown to sunrise only.

Because of a radio-telephone installation requiring constant attention, the front-light caisson was one of the last lighthouses on the bay to be manned by U.S. Coast Guard personnel. Accessible only by boat, the house on the main deck was reached by a steel ladder that was raised or lowered like a fire escape—difficult or impossible to climb in rough weather. In addition to the cupboard that housed the range light, the main deck was divided into three rooms—an engine room, a kitchen and a room that, incredibly, served as living and sleeping quarters as well as office and radio shack "It's so small," one of its keepers remarked in 1955, "every time you sneeze, you have to swab the place."

The silhouette of the front light of the Craighill Range is unmistakable. The top tier of the caisson's plates flare outward, increasing the diameter of the first level to support the 27-foot-diameter dwelling and a timber gallery deck with cast-iron balustrades bolted to iron brackets cantilevered from the top of the caisson. The balustrade posts, with capped round finials, are attached to each cantilevered bracket. Boat davits are placed at the northeast and southwest sides of the structure and the original privy is also visible extending from the main deck. At one time, a large fog bell was joined to the sloping circular roof of the first level. Eight windows are evenly spaced around the first-level living quarters and these windows and the front door, which faces north, have decorative cast-iron pediments. The second, or watch level, only 14 feet in diameter, supports the 10-sided lantern and its gallery.

Although, according to the Maryland Historical Trust's detailed report, much of the lighthouse remains in sound condition, work needs to be done to preserve and restore this lighthouse. Both the lower level, reached by descending a ship's ladder through a trap door just inside the entranceway (once used to store paint, oil, and the water which was drained from the roof into two 750-gallon tanks) and the first level have been open to the elements and used as a shelter and nesting site by birds. The watch level, reached by an enclosed spiral stairway (used also as a storage area for batteries), is damp and poorly ventilated. Throughout the structure, the walls and floors require refinishing.

The front light of the Craighill Range was automated in May of 1964—35 years after automation of the rear light—and together these two lights remain active as important navigational aids for mariners entering and leaving Baltimore Harbor.

Terry Corbett

Craighill Channel, Upper Range (The Cutoff Channel)

In March of 1885, an appropriation of $25,000 was secured by the Light-House Board for construction of range lights for a new cutoff between the Craighill and Brewerton Channels at the entrance to the Baltimore harbor. Shortly thereafter, official correspondence between the office of the U.S. Attorney General and Major Jared A. Smith, an engineer in the office of the 5th Light house district (and a man who left some memorable 19th-century photographs of Chesapeake Bay lighthouses), notes that one of the parcels of land which the Light-House Board wished to acquire was "part of a patented tract, the first recorded mention of which is the Patent dated January 29, 1666, from the Proprietary Government of Maryland to Solomon Sparrow, as follows:

> *This Patent grants the parcel of land called "Sparrows Nest" lying on the West side of Chesapeake Bay and the North side of Patapsco River. Beginning at the mouth of a creek in said river called Broad Creek and running South down the river one hundred and eighty perches in length to a marked persimmon tree upon the point called "Sparrows Point."*

By August of 1885, a site had been purchased for the rear beacon and the land deed approved and, by September of that year, work on both beacons and the keepers' dwellings was underway. (Keepers' lodgings for both the front and rear lights were built on shore—the rear tower is itself on shore and a wooden pier originally connected the front light to the shore near the keeper's house.)

The diminutive front tower of the Craighill Channel Upper Range, circa 1950. When the keeper took up residence here in 1893, the locomotive headlight then in use as the range light, had to be moved to the exterior of the tower. Photo, U.S. Coast Guard.

At first, it was planned to adapt the rear tower of the old North Point range as the front lighthouse of the Craighill Channel Upper Range (also referred to as the Cutoff Channel), but then the Board reported that, "careful examination showed it to be entirely unsuitable for the purpose." Instead, the Light-House Board decided to demolish the old tower and drew up plans "for a new tower, octagonal in shape, and built of brick, to stand upon the old stone foundation or pier, which is entirely secure." Thus, adding somewhat to the confusion of names, the front upper-range light is still sometimes referred to as the old North Point light. The fact of the matter is that the Craighill Channel lights, front and rear, upper and lower ranges, make much more sense in every way—architecturally, historically, and functionally—once one has seen the brilliant beacons line up on the approach to Baltimore Harbor by boat.

Construction of the rear tower proceeded smoothly. "The rear beacon," the Board reported, "consists of an inner wooden shaft, covered with corrugated iron and supported by an iron skeleton frame, forming a frustum of a square pyramid, resting on stone and brick foundation piers." Structurally, the architecturally unimposing tower appears to have undergone no change to the present day. The four-sided pyramidal iron frame and the square central shaft enclosing the stairway to the light is still painted white; the metal roof is brown. The height of the rear range light above mean high water is 64 feet, 39 feet above the light of the front range light.

Michael Ventura

Work at both sites was carried on simultaneously so that by January 15, 1886—though lacking the finishing touches, especially as regards keepers' amenities—the work had progressed sufficiently for the lights (initially, two locomotive headlights) to be exhibited for the first time. Work was then suspended until April "because of the difficulty in getting workmen and material to the station through the ice in the river and over the snow-clogged roads." In the spring, the keepers' dwellings and lighthouse grounds were graded, drained, fenced and painted and the stations were placed in fully habitable order. Problems came later for, oddly, within a few years of completion, there were difficulties with the rights-of-way to both keepers' dwellings.

In 1888, the Board noted in its annual report that the gates to the rear lightkeeper's house had been relocated because the adjoining property owner had "declined to allow the keeper to pass over his property any longer." "[T]he old gate opening was closed," the Board reported, "and the gate was repaired

FRONT LIGHT

Light station established:
1886

Location:
On pier formerly occupied by rear beacon of old North Point Range on the north side of the mouth of the Patapsco River. The range marks the cutoff channel between the Craighill and Brewerton channels, at the entrance to Baltimore Harbor.

Position:
39 11 49
76 26 55

Characteristic of Light:
Fixed red; lighted 24 hours a day.

Height of light, above mean high water:
15 feet.

Range:
Approximately 15 miles.

Description of Station:
Octagonal brick tower, painted in three horizontal bands, upper and lower, red; middle, white.

and moved to a position near the water line, opening on the right-of-way owned by the Government."

In 1890, the front lightkeeper's premises were spruced up with 450 feet of picket fencing, brick walkways and four new gates. The roof, gutters and downspouts of the house were repaired, wallpaper was removed and the walls were refinished with fresh paint. Finally, seventeen window screens and two screen doors were hung. "The station," the Board noted, "is now in excellent condition." Nevertheless, when, on August 28, 1893, a severe late-summer storm washed out the wooden bridge connecting the keeper's living quarters to the front beacon, and also submerged the right-of-way between the two, the Board decided that it was "best to fit the beacon for occupancy by the keeper rather than to undertake to rebuild the bridge and purchase a new right-of-way."

To make room on the diminutive lighthouse for the keeper, the locomotive headlight was moved from the interior to the exterior of the tower—a fact which gives a fairly accurate impression of just how cramped his quarters were. In addition, a boat landing and davits were installed, and the keeper was provided with a small boat to get him to and from the shore.

The 12-foot-square, front-light tower with truncated corners (giving the structure an octagonal appearance) and a pyramidal roof topped with a venti-

Michael Ventura

The rear light of the Craighill Channel Upper Range, circa 1950. Photo, U.S. Coast Guard.

lator ball, is—according to the Maryland Historical Trust's more recent report and measurements—22 feet in height.* The tower rests on a 30-foot-square stone masonry pier situated in the waters off Sparrows Point. Painted in three broad horizontal bands of equal width, two red and one white, its modest decorative features include a course of decorative brick at mid-section and molded brick arches around the front door and first-level windows. The lighthouse is difficult to reach because of large rocks just below the water line and boaters must generally view the lighthouse from some distance.

Both the front and rear Cutoff Channel lights were placed on unmanned operation in 1929 and all lighthouse personnel were removed.

* For the record, our research did not locate any records indicating that the front tower was torn down in the 1930's, nor that a previous 27-foot tower was replaced at that time with one of 18 feet, as reported by de Gast in 1973. The 1896 Light List describes an 18-foot tower; both the Maryland Historical Trust in 1992 and the 1994 *Light List* give a height of 22 feet. The discrepancy is probably quite simply because the earlier light list reports a height from the base of the tower to the center of the lantern and the latter measurements are from the base of the tower to the top of the lantern.

REAR LIGHT
Light station established:
1886

Location:
On mainland, head of Old Road Bay, 1.8 miles NNW. 1/2 W. from preceding (2600 yards, 329.5 degrees from front light).

Position:
39 12 58
76 27 47

Characteristic of Light:
Fixed red; lighted 24 hours a day.

Height of light, above mean high water:
74 feet.

Distance visible, in nautical miles:
18 miles.

Description of Station:
Four-sided, open iron-frame pyramid, with square central shaft, surmounted by a lantern. Framework and shaft painted white; lantern roof, brown, 56 feet from base of structure to center of lantern.

Seven Foot Knoll

On October 10, 1851, William Branford Shubrick, president of the newly constituted Light-House Board, wrote to the Secretary of the Treasury Thomas Corwin.

Sir: I have the honor to submit, herewith, plans, drawings, and specifications for a light-house on 'Seven-foot knoll,' in the Patapsco river, which have been carefully prepared by the Committee on Construction of Light-houses, and examined and approved by the board.

At this time, the development of the screwpile design offered new possibilities for the location of lighthouses on the bay, and the engineers were ambitious, recommending construction of a screwpile lighthouse with a height above high-water mark of 40 feet— "on the same principle as that erected at the Brandywine shoal."

After one of the foundation piles of Seven Foot Knoll was broken by heavy moving ice in the winter of 1884, the Light-House Board placed groups of ten oak piles about 50 feet from the lighthouse on all sides as an icebreaker. Ten years later the oak pilings had completely disappeared. Photo (c.1880's), Collection of Herb Entwistle.

Although the Seven Foot Knoll lighthouse, built in 1855, was only the second screwpile built on the Chesapeake Bay, it has outlasted all but three (Drum Point, Hooper Strait, and Thomas Point) of the more than 40 that were built on the bay. Fabrication of the original octagonal cast-iron lighthouse and its iron pilings was undertaken by a Baltimore iron foundry, Murray and Hazelhurst, that specialized in iron castings and machine building. The original cast-iron cottage—probably unique in lighthouse construction—was replaced by a round, wrought-iron plate dwelling sometime in the late 19th century.

In its day, iron-founding was on the cutting edge of industrial technology—giving industry and builders their first taste of the convenience of prefabricated parts. "The advantage of building the lighthouse from cast iron," according to Dennis Zembala, executive director of the Baltimore Museum of Industry, "was that the individual components of the structure—such as walls and beams—were carried to the site and assembled. This made construction much less difficult, especially when building out in the middle of the bay."

The first level of the circular dwelling, about eight feet above the octagonal service platform, has a diameter of 40 feet and is surrounded by a gallery deck, originally covered, five feet wide, with an iron handrail and balustrade. The second, or watch level, has a diameter of 15 feet, equal to the six-foot diameter lantern and nine-foot-wide lantern deck. The lantern, with 12 storm panels in the shape of truncated triangles, is also unique in overall design.

The area around the Seven Foot Knoll shoals, at the mouth of the Patapsco River, is renowned for dangerous wakes. Inevitably, too, strong currents, winds and heavy ice floes all took their toll on the lighthouse substructure. In 1884, the Light-House Board noted that "one of the piles of this structure was broken on January 19 by running ice."

To guard against further damage from this source, wooden piles were driven in bunches around the light-house as a temporary expedient; 150 piles in groups of 10 each, secured by strong iron cables, ... disposed in

28

Bill McAllen

a circle around the structure, each group being about 50 feet from the center pile of the light-house.

The following year, the damaged iron piling was replaced, but, again in 1894, the Board reported that,

[E]xamination of the substructure by a diver showed that all the water braces and some of the cast-iron sleeves to which they were secured had been broken by the movement of heavy masses of ice against the light-house.

The diver found that the foundation piles were "comparatively sound" but that "the clusters of oak piles placed around the light-house in 1884 as an ice breaker had disappeared." Concerned that the structure had been weakened, it was decided to deposit 790 cubic yards of riprap stone around the base "to strengthen it and receive the brunt of any future attacks by the ice."

Over the 133 years of its operation, many families lived on the lighthouse at Seven-foot Knoll. The lighthouse was manned until 1948. In May of that year, when the lighthouse was fully automated, *The Baltimore Sun* reported that the captain of the port, George E. McCabe was "much happier." "And he will be much happier," they continued, "when automatic lights have been put in all except five key lighthouses in the Chesapeake Bay." At that time, these five lighthouses were also radio stations that required attendants to operate the broadcasting equipment.

Light station established:
1855

Construction of present structure:
According to early Light Lists, the present iron structure (built around 1875) was preceded by a brown octagonal screwpile with green window shutters made of cast iron.

Location:
Pier 5 in Baltimore's Inner Harbor, Maryland.

Characteristic of light:
Inactive.

Description of station:
Circular screwpile constructed of iron plates, painted red; black lantern.

"Keepers are hard to get," McCabe told *The Baltimore Sun*. "Young people no longer want to live in lighthouses. And the oldtimers, who have been at it for years, are disappearing one by one." According to McCabe, even the coast guardsmen dreaded lighthouse duty. "Someone is always sick. Someone comes in to get the mail and has trouble with the boat. It's practically a rat race trying to keep all the lights going."

But other individuals recalled happier times at Seven-foot Knoll. In 1936, Knolie Bolling, daughter of James T. Bolling who lived at the Knoll from 1872 to 1879, recalled her life at the lighthouse where she was born on June 23, 1875, and after which she was named. "There are five large rooms," she said in an interview with *The Baltimore News* published on February 28, 1936, "and we had a piano and big bookcase with no end of books which occupied our time during the long winter evenings. Mother had been a school teacher and she taught us, because we had no way to get to and from the shore for school."

> *"Once when a storm blew up and prevented his return, my mother tended the light and rang the fog bell all night."*
>
> *"Part of our equipment was two small boats, and in good weather father would row to the nearest shore—six miles. We had nets and lines and an abundance of seafood, which we traded with the farmers for vegetables."*
>
> *"Under the living quarters we had a hog pen and chicken yard and there we kept our coal and wood. Several times our 'barnyard' was swept away by storms, but we always managed to rescue the livestock and keep them in our living quarters until father could rebuild their home. We even raised some vegetables in boxes on the big balcony, but it was hard work."*
>
> *In spring when the ice broke up, it would pile up against the lighthouse, rocking it and scattering our furniture around. That was what made us change our home finally."*

In fact, a few days before this interview appeared, *The Baltimore Sun* reported that "[a]dvancing before a northwest wind, more near-zero weather was expected ... to seize the Chesapeake Bay and Baltimore harbor in its icy grip." Shipping was halted and several boats had run aground or were stuck in the ice. "Movement of ice near the mouth of the harbor menaced two lighthouses," the article continued. "They were the front range-light of the Craighill Channel, around which ice was piled at a height estimated at thirty feet, and the Seven-Foot Knoll light, which was not visible from the observatory of the Maritime Exchange."

The family of Thomas J. Steinhise, the last civilian keeper at Seven Foot Knoll, has also collected many memories of his sojourn, beginning in 1919. Steinhise's family did not live at the light but he had eight days of shore leave every month. Working with one other keeper, each spent eight days alone at the lighthouse while the other took shore leave once a month. According to Steinhise, his job required the skills of a painter, carpenter, navigator and information clerk. An ability to cook, he added, was also an important qualification. Steinhise is especially remembered for the heroic rescue of the five-man crew of the tug Point Breeze which sank in the vicinity of the light on August 21, 1933. "He braved very high seas," his granddaughter Bernadette

Gesser recalled, "in a launch with a faulty motor, to save the men of the tug from the raging waters. As a result of his courage, he was awarded a Congressional Medal for Heroism." Unfortunately, the engineer of the Point Breeze died from exposure soon after the rescue.

In 1982, John R. Walters, then a lieutenant assigned to the U.S. Coast Guard Cutter Sledge, reported that Seven Foot Knoll's appearance was "grim."

> *The foundation appears to be wasted badly enough to justify demolition of the light.... When we arrived the door to the lighthouse was open... Graffiti was everywhere but the lantern and light were undamaged. At the intersection of the boiler-plate exterior walls with the main deck, and on the second deck, there was severe wastage of metal—about 80-90% has wasted away; 90-95% of the plating on the roof has washed away, exposing the concrete substructure.*

Declared surplus property by the U.S. Coast Guard when it was replaced by a steel tower in the late 1980's, the City of Baltimore was able to obtain title to the lighthouse and permission to move it to Pier 5 as part of its harbor redevelopment. On a cold clear day in October 1988, in choppy waters with gusting 35-knot-per-hour winds, the first attempt was made to remove the 220-ton lighthouse from its iron pilings on the knoll and, suspended in a sling from a huge derrick (nicknamed "The Samson"), to barge it up the Patapsco seven miles to its new home at the foot of Pier 5 in Baltimore's Inner Harbor. In spite of the rough weather, the president of Empire Construction (which had coordinated the move) was excited and optimistic. "This is a half-million dollar job that took two months to plan but will be carried out in less than one day," he said confidently.

All eyes are on the lighthouse as it is slowly lifted from its severed pilings in October of 1988 to be barged up the Patapsco to its new home on Pier 5 of the Baltimore Inner Harbor. Today the refurbished lighthouse is seen by millions of visitors each year. Photo, Terry Corbett.

Actually, the move took two days, though it was no less remarkable in its execution. According to one observer, "Divers dressed against the cold had trouble severing the pilings because of the wind—every time they would be in position on one of the rocks and ready to fire up their special torches, waves would crash over them and they would have to begin over again."

Logistically, one of the most difficult maneuvers was transporting the lighthouse under the Key Bridge. "We researched all the different aspects of the move," the executive vice-president of The Empire Construction Company noted, "but there were still some tense moments... Our calculations told us that we had to lower the height of the derrick by 30 feet to pass under the bridge. Thirty feet may sound like a lot of room to play with, but it isn't when you're bouncing about on the water trying to guide a 185-foot structure that has a 220-ton, 133-year-old lighthouse hanging from it, going upstream, under a bridge."

When the lighthouse arrived at Pier 5, it still bore a sign that read "DANGER. Heavy wake area. No anchoring within 500 yds. of this structure."

The move cost $600,000, and, with expenditures totaling another $100,000, the Seven Foot Knoll lighthouse has now been restored as a visitor's center and serves as the offices of The Living Classrooms Foundation. It is open to the public and its condition, according to the Maryland Historic Trust's 1991 report, is good. The first level, formerly the living quarters of the keeper (two bedrooms, a living room and kitchen) now contains historical displays for thousands of visitors and participants in educational programs:

31

Baltimore Light

With the exception of Chesapeake Light, a skeletal tower built to replace the Chesapeake Lightship in 1964, Baltimore Light is one of only four lighthouses built in the Chesapeake Bay during the 20th century (the others are Hooper Island, 1901, Point No Point, 1902 and Thimble Shoal, 1914). First commissioned in 1908, the construction of Baltimore Light represents the end of an era, for, shortly after its completion, the thrust towards fully automated beacons and unmanned stations began in earnest. Perhaps, then, it is not surprising that the Light-House Board's original

request for $60,000 for a light to mark the entrance to the Baltimore channel at the mouth of the Magothy River was made in 1890, a full 18 years before the light was commissioned. The Board knew that it was going to be a difficult job. "On account of the impressible character of the shoal, and the liability to damage or destruction by fields of moving ice," the Board stated, "no light-house, other than an expensive one, can be made permanent."

On August 18, 1894, Congress appropriated the requested sum and careful evaluation of the selected site was undertaken. The results, as reported in 1895, were disappointing.

Borings made at the new site selected for this light-house, have shown that there is a layer of soft mud extending 55 feet below the surface of the shoal. ... The great depth to which a structure will have to be sunk makes the problem of erecting a light-house within the limits of the amount appropriated by Congress... somewhat difficult.

Greg Pease

When, in 1899, an attempt was made to plant an experimental disk pile at the chosen site, it was clear that completion of the project would require additional funding. "It is now evident," the Board stated, "that the expense of building a light-station in the 55 feet of semifluid mud which overlays the sandy bottom will... cost $60,000, in addition to the $60,000 already appropriated." The recommendation was renewed in 1900 and again in 1901. Finally, in June 1902 authorization for completion of the station was received from Congress.

In 1903, the bidding process was opened, but only one contractor came forward—and his bid was another $80,000 above the $120,000 then appropriated. The offer was rejected. A new bidding process was begun and the lowest bid accepted. The metal work for the lighthouse was completed in September 1904, and, according to the annual report of the Light-House Board, the wooden caisson was towed to the site on September 19. It was an inauspicious beginning. "On the 21st heavy seas filled the cylinder which... caused it to settle to one side, about 7 feet out of level. The bottom of the caisson was then about on an average 8 feet below the surface of the shoal." The contractor withdrew to make repairs and as-

From 1964 to 1966, Baltimore Light was powered by a small atomic generator. This photo was taken on May 20, 1964, the day the 4,600-pound generator was installed. It was, the Coast Guard later noted, "an idea that was never pursued beyond the experimental stage..." Photo, U.S. Coast Guard.

In 1908, Baltimore Light was finally completed and commissioned, four years after the caisson foundation was towed to the site and lowered into the bay where, unfortunately, it tipped completely onto its side. The original contractor never returned and the difficult task of righting the caisson was successfully undertaken by the insurance company. Photo, U.S. Coast Guard.

semble additional materials but, when he resumed work in October, "during a severe storm, the structure turned over flat on its side." Once again the contractor withdrew—this time permanently.

In 1906 the Board observed that "the wrecked caisson of this light-house is now lying on its side at the site in apparently the same condition as when abandoned by the contractor on October 12, 1904." Legal complications soon followed. The government sued the contractor, and in 1905, the insurance company undertook to complete the project. It was a mammoth job.

A pier was built around the lighthouse, temporary quarters for workmen and storage areas were constructed on the pier, and "a large boiler, a hoisting engine, 3 compressors, 3 air receivers, 3 water tanks, and a steam pump" were taken out to the site. The report continued:

A mast for a derrick was erected and guyed, and the boom was framed ... A pipe line for steam has been run under the north side, and another for air has been carried under the south side of the pier. An artesian well has been sunk 179 feet below high water.

Initially, wire cables carrying heavy weights were secured to the caisson and "led over timber A-frames and booms projecting 50 feet beyond its outer edge." The weights succeeded in bringing the caisson about 45 degrees towards the vertical. Then the weights were readjusted and the caisson was righted another 10 degrees. The Board continued:

Pumps were then set up on the pier, and by means of these mud was removed from under the high side of the caisson. With this assistance, and under the weight on the A-frames and the strain on the tackles, the caisson moved slowly until...it had reached a position only about 17 degrees from the vertical. The following spring, the third course of cylinder plates was bolted into place. Eighty tons of large stone was placed in the compartment on the high side of the caisson, mud was pumped from under that side, a strain was taken on the tackles, and the top of the upper course of cylinder plates on the...high side, moved to the eastward about 5 feet 2 inches.

When finally finished, there were six courses of cylinder plates and the caisson had been "carried down to a level of 82 feet below high water."

In 1908 the Light-House Board reported that "the righting of the caisson and the sinking of the foundation cylinder into its required position have been performed with remarkable success." The light was commissioned on October 1, 1908.

The caisson foundation of Baltimore Light flares out from a 30-foot diameter to accommodate a 24-by-24-foot two-story brick house with truncated corners (giving the building an octagonal appearance) and main gallery. The third, or watch level, is formed by a timber-framed mansard roof which, in turn, supports the lantern deck and eight-sided, timber-framed lantern with a copper roof, roof lining and ventilator ball.

34

In 1964, Baltimore Light became the first atomic-powered lighthouse in the world. A 60-watt isotopic power generator was developed by the Martin Company in a joint effort with the U.S. Coast Guard and the Atomic Energy Commission (now the Department of Energy). *The Evening Sun* reported that the generator was "smaller than a 55-gallon oil drum," and that it would "supply a continuous flow of electricity...for ten years without refueling." In fact, however, the small nuclear reactor was removed two years later—"an idea," the Coast Guard reported, "that was never pursued beyond the experimental stage due to cost and environmental considerations."

Unmanned operation, however, began to take its toll on the sturdy structure. In 1983 Baltimore Light was inspected in preparation for execution of the Coast Guard's "Operation Spruce Up." The gloomy report of then-lieutenant John R. Walters itemized the damage.

> *Extensive water damage to walls, ceilings and floors... Several port holes on the caisson were open to the weather... No windows were sealed—pigeons and weather have free access to the interior of the structure...the situation has existed for several years. Guano was several inches thick on all decks and even the stairway. Fledglings and eggs were found throughout the structure... Holes in the roof allowed water into the lighthouse interior. All lantern room panes had bullet holes in them. The lens was also bullet punctured... There are cracks in the masonry exterior... The wooden door has met its share of vandals and needs to be replaced with a steel frame/door. .... At some time someone tried to burn the lighthouse interior. In addition to water damage, termite damage is evident. One boiler plate section has a vertical crack about one inch wide, running the entire length of the plate. The lightning arrestor was adorned with various beer cans.*

Repairs were soon made. The windows were bricked, the ladders secured and placed out of reach, a steel door and frame were installed, acrylic panes replaced the storm glass in the lantern, and, it was hoped, that the light was once again secure from vandals.

A 1988 report made by the commanding officer of the Coast Guard Cutter Red Birch reflects the Coast Guard's growing concern for the historical integrity of the lighthouse. "I have included in my recommendations," the officer informed the Commander of the Fifth Coast Guard District, "[plans] to prepare and paint the boat davits and the 'outhouse' outboard of the rails on the caisson. While these no longer serve any function, they are in nearly original condition, and are part of the external structure which may have historic significance."

In 1989 and 1990, the U.S. Coast Guard Cutter Red Birch completed several badly needed maintenance projects and repairs. The masonry was prepped, caulked and painted—the caisson was sandblasted and painted. Reproductions of the original boarding ladders were fabricated and installed. The yellowed acrylic storm panels in the lantern were replaced with clear safety glass and the rotten timbers of the interior lantern floor were replaced with tongue-and-groove flooring and given three coats of varnish. Brass components to the lantern were renewed and repaired. "We are most proud," the commanding officer of the Red Birch reported back to the Fifth District headquarters, "of the ... Baltimore Light lantern gallery repairs."

Light station established:
1908

Construction of present structure:
1908

Location:
In approximately 23 feet of water, west of the south entrance to the Craighill Channel, at the entrance to Baltimore Harbor, on the west side of the north end of the Chesapeake Bay.

Position:
39 03 (36)
76 24 (52)

Characteristic of light:
Flashing white, 2.5 second intervals; red sector from 082 to 150 degrees.

Height of light, above mean high water:
52 feet.

Range:
White, 7 miles; red, 5 miles.

Description of station:
Brown cylindrical foundation pier expanding in trumpet shape at its upper end; white octagonal two-story brick dwelling with mansard roof; black lantern.

Sandy Point Shoal

In 1857, the Light-House Board obtained title to a small parcel of land at Sandy Point on the west side of the Chesapeake Bay and a keeper's dwelling was constructed with a lantern on the roof containing a diminutive fifth-order Fresnel lens. The light was commissioned in 1858 and in 1863 a fog bell was added to the installation. Nevertheless, by the mid-1870's it was found to be wholly inadequate to mark the shoals which by now extended almost one mile into the bay. Because of its distance from the main channel, both the light and the fog bell were useless to ships drawing more than 10 feet of water, and the shortcomings of Sandy Point light became ever more apparent as steamer traffic on the bay increased. "Nearly all the passenger steamers running into the port of Baltimore from below, of which there are many," the Light-House Board reported in 1874, "change their course at this point, and this becomes a hazardous undertaking to boats crowded with passengers and running on time, when neither the light can be seen nor the fog-bell heard." The Board recommended construction of a new lighthouse, of screwpile design, on the outer edge of the shoal.

In ensuing years, as commerce and passenger traffic on the bay continued to expand, the Board's request was repeated annually—and with increasing urgency. Finally, in 1882, an appropriation for $25,000 was obtained but, unfortunately, the appropriation was not sufficient for construction of the proposed lighthouse. When an additional $15,000 was requested and refused, the Board reported that it had gone ahead with alternative plans.

This photo was taken shortly after construction of Sandy Point light. Freezing salt spray soon required the Light-House Board to take measures to protect the brick with several coats of paint. Photo, National Archives.

Rather than delay the work longer, it was decided to erect a less expensive tower... This is a cylindrical iron caisson, 35 feet in diameter, and 32 feet 6 inches high, filled with concrete and resting on the shoal.

Construction was begun in August of 1883 and the light was exhibited October 30 of the same year. The Board's breathless description of the erection of the lighthouse is interesting and shows no little conceit regarding their efficiency (as opposed, perhaps, to that of the U.S. Congress), their state-of-the-art technology, and their managerial know-how:

On August 11 the working party and material for commencing the erection of the house arrived at the site. The driving of the piles for the platform, on which to rest the caisson before lowering it, was at once commenced, and was finished on the 14th, and the outer or working platform was in position on the 18th. The derrick mast, boom, concrete-mixer, boiler, and engine were then placed on it on the 20th; the inner platform for supporting the caisson was constructed on the 23d; the first section of the caisson was put together on the 24th and lowered on the 25th, the second section being placed on the 27th. The two sections were then sunk into the sand 3 feet and leveled by means of a water-jet and force pump. Quarters 20 by 31 feet and a kitchen 16-feet square were meanwhile constructed, and a plank walk was laid to the shore, and

Dave Harp

Light station established:
1858

Construction of present structure:
1883

Location:
In approximately 13 feet of water, approximately 1000 yards out on the shoal extending out from Sandy Point State Park beach, one and a half miles north of the Chesapeake Bay Bridge, on the west side of the Chesapeake Bay, Maryland.

Position:
39 01 (52)
76 23 (08)

Characteristic of light:
Flashing white, six second intervals.

Height of light, above mean high water:
51 feet.

Range:
9 miles.

Description of station:
Red brick dwelling with white roof on brown cylindrical foundation.

Fog signal:
Horn: 1 blast every 30 seconds (3-second blast); operates continuously from September 15 to June 1.

material for concrete—stone, gravel, cement, and sand—was also landed on the platform. The work of filling in the concrete was commenced on August 31 and completed on September 26, about 1,000 cubic yards being mixed and placed in the caisson during that time. The third section of the iron caisson was bolted on September 15. Frames were made and covered with boards for forming the concrete around the cellar, and a brick pier was built in the cellar for the center column. The construction of the brick-work, of which the tower is principally composed, was commenced on September 27 and completed on October 9. The erection of the lantern was commenced on October 10 and finished on the 11th, with the exception of the putting in of the glass, which was done within the week. The house was ready for the exhibition of the light on October 18, though some finishing work and painting remained to be done. To admit of due notice to mariners, however, the light was not exhibited until October 30, 1883.

The three-story brick masonry and timber-framed dwelling is 24 by 24 feet with truncated corners that give the building an octagonal shape. A distinctive sloping mansard roof (with peaked dormer windows and arched window-glass frames) supports the octagonal timber-framed lantern and lantern deck with iron railings and balustrades. A decorative course of brickwork between the first and second levels and a bracketed wooden cornice add the charm of a Victorian townhouse to the lighthouse dwelling. The first and second masonry levels were designed as living quarters for the keepers, the third timber-framed level as a watch area. Additionally, a lower level in the caisson itself, accessible by a wooden ship's ladder, was used for the storage of coal, water and oil and contains a masonry pier built to support the hollow iron column which at one time accommodated the counterweights of the fog bell's winding mechanism.

In 1890 a fixed light was substituted for the flashing light that had traditionally identified Sandy Point. The boat-hoisters were repaired and the walls of the keeper's dwelling, which were faced with pressed brick and molded brick ornamentation, were painted to prevent erosion.

Still appearing much as it did in the 1890's, the Sandy Point light was electrified in 1929 (when the fixed light was once again changed to a flashing light) and fully automated on May 14, 1963. Without personnel, the easily accessible lighthouse fell prey to vandals. In June of 1979, a coastguardsman found the Sandy Point lighthouse "vandalized beyond repair." Only shattered parts of the handmade 19th-century crystal lens remained—apparently senselessly destroyed by someone swinging a baseball bat. The light was replaced with an acrylic lens and the Coast Guard offered a reward for information leading to the arrest and conviction of the culprits, pointing disconsolately to innumerable acts of vandalism to navigational aids on the bay that threatened the safety of mariners.

In 1988, 1989 and 1990 the Coast Guard undertook major repairs and some restoration work at Sandy Point. For example, in 1990 the Coast Guard replaced the original tin cornices with mahogany cornices carefully designed to replicate the originals and repainted the entire structure. Even so, both the U.S. Coast Guard and the Maryland Historical Trust identify much additional work that needs to be done to stabilize, preserve and restore Sandy Point (the

Maryland Historical Trust's 1991 report estimates a price tag of approximately $90,000). On the exterior, a large crack in the caisson plates near the boarding ladder needs to be sealed and the severely cracked gallery deck needs to be replaced to prevent water from entering the iron and concrete interface of the caisson. On the dwelling's exterior, crumbling bricks and missing window trim require replacement and point work. Moisture penetration, though evidently now under control, has caused extensive damage to the interior of the lighthouse and all woodwork and plaster surfaces are in need of refinishing.

Because of its visibility from both sides of the Chesapeake Bay Bridge and its location only 1000 yards from the Sandy Point State Park beach (visited by over half a million people annually) in one of the pleasure-boat capitals of the Chesapeake Bay, the lighthouse, which is still an active navigational aid, will almost certainly remain an object of public education and interest. The Maryland Historical Trust's report suggests, for example, that Sandy Point light might easily be incorporated into a tour of adjacent bay lighthouses (including perhaps Thomas Point and Baltimore lights) in the further development of state-run recreational and educational programs dealing with the history and ecology of the Chesapeake Bay.

Thomas Point Shoal

Since 1824, when Congress first appropriated $6,000 for construction of a light at Thomas Point, three consecutive lighthouses have marked the shoal extending from the north side of South River, four miles south of the entrance to Annapolis Harbor. The original tower was constructed by John Donahoo on a seven-acre parcel of land purchased for $529.69, but this lighthouse—Donahoo's first—proved his inexperience and had to be rebuilt little more than a decade later. The new tower, constructed in 1838 by Winslow Lewis (who was, in fact, a building associate of Donahoo's), remained standing until 1894, although in 1875 it was replaced with a screwpile lighthouse located well out on the shoal.

For many the signature lighthouse of the Chesapeake Bay, Thomas Point Shoal was manned until 1986. It is the only screwpile that remains in its original location on the waters of the bay. Photo, Collection P. Hornberger.

"It will be observed," the Light-House Board reported in 1872, "...that the light-house at Thomas's Point...can serve but poorly its purpose as a warning of the dangerous shoal that makes out from it at a distance of one and one-quarter miles into the bay." The Board's report noted that "[u]nder no circumstances can vessels drawing more than 8 feet of water pass within one and a quarter miles of it, as the shoal is continuous, and has on it only that depth at the outer extremity." The Board observed that complaints from mariners were frequent and that both a lighthouse and fog bell were needed to remedy a "defect long felt by the commerce of the Chesapeake Bay." Last but not least, the 1838 tower was in a terrible state of repair: "The rain, in windy weather, beats through the old masonry of the tower, flooding the inside of the structure, and frequently damaging the material in charge of the keeper."

The following year, the Light-House Board reported that Congress had made an appropriation of $20,000 for the light but that "because the location on the extreme point of the shoal is one of great exposure," special plans were being drawn up that meant an additional $25,000 would be needed to complete the structure. At this time, in growing dismay at the inability of screwpile structures to withstand the onslaught of moving ice, the Light-House Board apparently favored a caisson-like structure for the site—referred to in this instance as "a cast-iron tube filled with concrete."

The tube will be of the form of a frustum of a cone to a height of 12 feet from the bottom; above this, it will be cylindrical...[t]he shell will be built up in sections, bolted together through stout flanges and sunk in position by filling it with concrete.

The request was repeated in 1874, but this time the amount requested was considerably less—only an additional $15,000. Finally, in 1875, the Light-House Board reported that the appropriation had been received though, in the end, the original and less-expensive screwpile structure had been decided upon. In fact, proposals for furnishing the ironwork had already been published and awarded. "This work," the Board observed, "is now progressing well, and it is expected that the structure will be finished during the present season."

Rick Brady

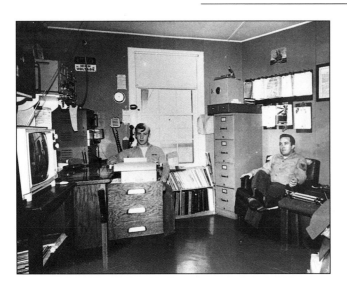

Whereas early lighthouse keepers found entertainment in the book collections provided by the Light-House Board, the Coast Guard keepers of the 1960's turned to television to wile away their lonely hours. Chesapeake Bay Maritime Museum, Photo, C.C. Harris.

Thomas Point Shoal kitchen, 1968. Chesapeake Bay Maritime Museum, Photo, C. C. Harris.

True to their word, the light was exhibited for the first time on November 20, 1875, and the light in the old masonry tower was discontinued.

Located at the mouth of the South River, a short boat ride from Annapolis, the Thomas Point lighthouse, designed by engineers of the U.S. Light-House Board, is architecturally (with only minor alterations) probably the finest example of a screwpile cottage anywhere in the world—and it will surely endure, as well, as a symbol of late-19th and early-20th-century life on the Chesapeake Bay. (For example, the Thomas Point lighthouse has recently been adopted as the emblem of the Chesapeake Chapter of the U.S. Lighthouse Society.)

The dwelling is a compact hexagonal structure, 35 feet in diameter, which sits on seven piles, six of which are spaced at 60-degree intervals around the perimeter of the central piling. The finely proportioned house is adorned with carefully crafted details such as the carved balusters of the six-sided walkway that surround both the cottage and the widow's walk of the lantern gallery 43 feet above the bay. The molded wood siding of the frame house is painted white, its tin roof red, and the octagonal lantern and catwalk were at one time both painted black (the lantern gallery is now white). Six dormers are tucked neatly into the sloping hexagonal first-story roof and the interior of both the first and second levels is lined with beaded four-inch-wide Philadelphia board, painted in light colors. The flooring is diagonally laid, random-width Georgia pine and the interior stairway connecting the first and second levels winds around a central wooden column and is set into a hexagonal shaft.

In the winter of 1877, the foundation of the new lighthouse was damaged by heavy ice floes and "a detached ice-breaker" had to be placed about 90 feet from the lighthouse. "This ice-breaker," the Board explained, "consists of three wrought-iron screw-piles, connected together by double channel-iron beams, surmounted by heavy cast-iron caps, securely bolted together." The impact of the ice, the Board reported, had overturned and damaged the lens so that its replacement was necessary. Meanwhile, for a few weeks, a beacon was once again lit in the old Thomas Point tower. Between 1886 and 1887, some 1600 cubic yards of riprap stone were placed around the lighthouse—still clearly visible at low tide—and in 1899, new-model fourth-order lamps were supplied.

By 1964, the Thomas Point light was the only manned lighthouse on the bay. Four coastguardsmen alternated duty with three of them at the station at all times. Each remained at the station for 21 days and then went ashore for seven days. Once a month, a lightship tender delivered water, fuel and other provisions. In the 1970's this routine was changed. A crew of only three with two weeks on, one week off, left two men at the station at all times. The new man arrived on Tuesdays, bringing the mail and groceries for the week—and the man going off duty took the previous weeks' garbage ashore. According to Boatswain's Mate Richard Sapp, who was assigned to the lighthouse in the mid-1960's, it was "a good duty." "We keep busy with the equipment," he said, "and we are a calibration station for all the ship traffic that moves on the bay." But he couldn't imagine lighthouse life without television. "I don't know what lighthouse men did late at night, especially a clear night, before television. We see the late show, and the late, late show and the late, late, late show." In the early 1980's, Fireman Apprentice Scott Kaufman, a junior member of the four-man crew also commented philosophically about the loneliness of lighthouse duty. "There's a lot of time to think. All the problems you have. You can just sit out here and think out all the angles. I'll even sit here and think about my friends' problems. That's how much time I have."

In 1972, tropical storm Agnes threw 23-foot waves against the structure, occasioning some superficial damage. But it was a political storm rather than the tail end of a hurricane that proved decisive for the future of Thomas Point lighthouse. That same year, the U.S. Coast Guard quietly announced that Thomas Point light was one of approximately 100 lighthouse structures being "evaluated for cost effectiveness," (a term that the public immediately recognized as something of a Coast Guard euphemism for the pending destruction of a light—at least in the case of screwpile cottages that were easily burned, conveniently leaving their iron infrastructures intact for the erection of steel towers). When news was broadcast in local papers that the U.S. Coast Guard was considering dismantling the structure and replacing it with a steel skeleton tower, the public outcry was instantaneous and loud. Soon, the banner to save the lighthouse was taken up by regional, state and national politicians. It was, after all (as *Evening Sun* reporter Jeff Valentine wryly observed at the time), an election year, and the struggle for custody of the then-99-year-old Thomas Point light quickly became the rallying cry of many seeking political office. Inevitably, as politicians cruised to and from the lighthouse on information-gathering tours, the Coast Guard began to back down on its proposal to replace the lighthouse structure. On January 23, 1975, the light was declared an historic landmark.

Although the lighthouse is in generally excellent condition, the Maryland Historical Trust recommends restoration and repairs to the lighthouse at a cost of approximately $100,000. Because it is the last remaining screwpile on the bay, and because it continues as the lighthouse of greatest recognition on the Chesapeake Bay, the complete restoration and preservation of Thomas Point Shoal light is important to many. Over the years, some bids for use of the lighthouse have been forthcoming—for example, from the Smithsonian Environmental Research Institute which at one time expressed an interest in using the site as part of its educational program on the bay, but to date no permanent use arrangements have been made other than its primary purpose as a navigational aid to ship traffic on the bay.

Light station established:
1824

Construction of present structure:
1875

Location:
In approximately 8 feet of water, on the shoal making out from Thomas Point, on the west side of the Chesapeake Bay, Maryland, at the entrance to South River.

Position:
38 53 (57)
76 26 (10)

Characteristic of light:
Flashing white, 6 second intervals; 2 red sectors, marking the shoals off Thomas Point, from 011 to 051.5 degrees and from 096.5 to 202 degrees.

Height of light, above mean high water:
43 feet.

Range:
White sector, 13 miles; red sector, 11 miles.

Description of station:
White hexagonal screwpile cottage; piles and roof brown, lantern black.

Fog signal:
Horn: 1 blast every 15 seconds (2-second blast).

Hooper Strait

Recorded maritime history of the district now known as Hooper Strait begins in 1608 when Captain John Smith and his crew were caught in the vicinity during a severe storm. Limbo Straits was the picturesque name that Smith gave to the channel during this first expedition into the Chesapeake Bay. European settlement of the region began in the early 17th century (at this time the Straits District of Dorchester County encompassed an area, including Bloodsworth Island, renowned as the retreat of pirates).

The first lighthouse at Hooper Strait replaced one of many light vessels destroyed during the Civil War. The light-vessel station was established in 1827 and showed a fixed white light with a focal plane of 34 feet that was visible for 10 miles. The last light vessel at Hooper Strait was built in 1845. In 1867, a lighthouse of screwpile design was constructed in nine feet of water on the north side of the entrance into Tangier Sound marking the shoal on

the north side of the channel between the mainland and Bloodsworth Island. The first screwpile structure stood for only ten years before succumbing to heavy moving ice. The report of lighthouse keeper John S. Cornwell, dated January 24, 1877, describes the harrowing escape that he and his assistant, Alexander S. Conway, made from the cottage after it was shorn from its foundation.

On Monday night Jan'y 8th 1877 the wind was blowing from North-West and caused a large body of ice to pile up against the Light house, and it remained in that condition until the 11th inst. at which time about noon on that day the wind prevailing fresh from the South and at high water, the tide just beginning to eb [sic] the map of ice which was piled up against the house and other ice coming down on it caused the Iron Sleeve and the bolts to give way which supported the braces, in consequence of which there being nothing to support the house it began to Settle down rapidly in the water to the roof. The house remained in that position until Friday afternoon when it began to move out towards the Bay. The house Settled so rapidly that Capt. Conway nor myself had any time whatever to save any of the government property within the building—In fact we did not have time to Save anything but our-selves—not even our appearel [sic] only what we had on.

We escaped from our perilous condition by the aid of one of the boats belonging to the house which we pulled on the ice. We remained on the ice for twenty-four hours with the boat, exposed to the elements without any thing to shelter us, in consequence of which exposure both of us became frostbitten the effects of which we are now suffering, but much better than at first. When resqued [sic] by Captain Murphy of Billy's Island we had to abandon the boat on the ice, as she was so heavy we could do nothing with her.

The lighthouse keeper went on to apologize for failure to submit his quarterly report. "My returns for the quarter ending Dec 31st 1876 were all made out," he wrote, "but it was impossible to get them to the Post Office to send to you—when the house went down the papers went with it." Even so, the keeper and his assistant were apparently eager to take on another station: "Should there be another house erected, or a boat place in the site of the old one, Capt. Conway and myself will be ready to take charge of it..." In an attempt to salvage government property, two lighthouse tenders, the Tulip and the Heliotrope, were later sent to locate the lighthouse (it was found five miles south of Hooper Strait, sunk in water to its roof line) and were able to remove the lens, lamp and bell before floating ice endangered their salvage operation.

Shown in its original open water location, this cottage was built in 1880 to replace a lighthouse that succumbed to a mass of moving ice in 1879. In 1966, the lighthouse was once again threatened with destruction—this time Coast Guard demolition—when it was fortunately acquired by the Chesapeake Bay Maritime Museum. Photo, The Chesapeake Bay Maritime Museum.

Bill McAllen

45

Light station established:
1827

Construction of present structure:
1879

Location:
Chesapeake Bay Maritime Museum, St. Michaels, Maryland.

Characteristic of light:
Inactive.

Description of station:
White hexagonal screwpile cottage with a black lantern.

In January, 1879, Congress approved an appropriation for a second lighthouse and a white hexagonal screwpile structure supported by seven solid-iron piles, painted brown, with a brown roof and black lantern, was completed at a cost of $20,000. The cottage dwelling was constructed at the Lazaretto Depot in Baltimore, dismantled and, together with the ironwork, shipped on a schooner to the building site in September. Piles were driven 25 feet into the shoal and thereafter assembly time was very brief. "The screwing down of the piles was commenced on September 21," the Light-House Board reported in 1880. "The piles were placed in their position without any difficulty, the struts, tension bars, and sockets were fitted in place, and the wooden frame of the house was raised. The structure was ready for lighting early in October and on October 15, 1879, its light shone for the first time." The light exhibited was fixed white of the fifth order. In 1882 a red sector was introduced as an additional guide around shoals in the channel entering Tangier Sound.

On December 2, 1954, the light was fully automated and converted to unmanned status by the U.S. Coast Guard. The windows were boarded up. With minimum maintenance and no protection from vandals, the condition of the cottage inevitably began to deteriorate. By 1958, the Coast Guard had initiated a policy of complete removal of screwpile dwellings. Generally, the cottages were simply burned, concrete decks and small concrete battery houses were laid on the screwpile foundation (which was strengthened by the replacement of the radial and perimeter beams with new steel beams), and a skeletal structure was erected to show the light at the same elevation above mean high water as the original lantern. Thus it was that Hooper Strait light was slated for imminent destruction in 1966 when it was acquired by the fledgling Chesapeake Bay Maritime Museum in St. Michaels, 40 miles up the bay. The hexagonal lighthouse, 44 feet in diameter, was still in good condition overall, though it lacked paint and vandals had knocked off some of the gallery railings.

In spite of hemming and hawing on the part of the Coast Guard, acquisition of Hooper Strait light proved relatively easy for the Chesapeake Bay Maritime Museum (especially in comparison to the obstacles encountered by the Calvert Marine Museum when it sought acquisition of the Drum Point lighthouse). Although as late as July 1966, the U.S. Coast Guard stated in a letter to the museum that "this matter is currently in the planning stage and it is not anticipated that invitation for bids for this project will be released in the near future," three months later, on October 25, 1966, a final contract was negotiated between The Historical Society of Talbot County and The Arundel Corporation. The work of transporting the lighthouse was begun immediately. Besides the $12,500 that The Historical Society raised for the move, The Arundel Corporation received approximately $14,000 from the U.S. Treasury Department—the estimated cost of demolishing the lighthouse.

Pile Drivers, Inc. of Baltimore was contracted to build a new foundation at the Chesapeake Bay Maritime Museum. Tubular steel piles, 37-feet long, were supplied and delivered at cost by the Union Metal Company of Baltimore. These were then driven to a depth of 28 feet and filled with concrete. The square steel bearing plates were donated by the Easton Steel Company and the eight-inch steel beams were a gift of the Chase Steel Company. Con-

By 1966, when the Chesapeake Bay Maritime Museum acquired Hooper Strait light, neglect and vandalism had taken their toll on the cozy clapboard cottage. The lighthouse was barged 40 miles up the bay to its new home. Photo, The Chesapeake Bay Maritime Museum.

struction was begun on October 28 and completed four days later, one week before the lighthouse—cut in half just below the eaves, and from its foundation just below the first-level framing—arrived at its new location on Navy Point. Though unusually high seas and high winds delayed transportation of the lighthouse, not a pane of glass in the lantern cupola or the house itself was cracked or broken when, on November 9, 1966, the lighthouse was delivered and placed on the new foundation.

The lighthouse is now beautifully restored and is perhaps the most popular attraction at the Chesapeake Bay Maritime Museum. Although there are some regrets—for example, that the original solid cast-iron foundation had to be abandoned in place, that the lighthouse is not sitting in water, and that the new roof was made of copper and therefore cannot be painted red like the original tin roof—there are also plans to amplify historical interpretation of the lighthouse itself, focusing more specifically on the social history of lighthouse keepers and their families and on the bay commerce which their vigilance served. Hooper Strait light is one of only four remaining screwpile structures of the more than 40 that were built on the Chesapeake Bay.

Bloody Point Bar

Situated off the tip of Kent Island, near one of the deepest shipping channels of the bay—where the water reaches depths of up to 174 feet and the sides of the channel rise steeply to the shoals off Poplar Island—both the name and the ruddy-brown color of Bloody Point light seem particularly well chosen. From colonial times, there are gory tales from this Kent Island point—whispers of a grim massacre (it is said that English colonists lured a group of Indians there under a false pretense of friendship and murdered them) and rumors of the hanging of a ruthless French pirate. In more recent times, the light exploded in a raging fire that nearly cost two coastguardsmen their lives.

In 1868, recommendations forwarded by the engineer and inspector of the Fifth District to the Light-House Board for the erection of a light station at Bloody Point were approved and requests for an appropriation were inserted into the Board's annual report, but it was not until 1881, a full thirteen years later, that a $25,000 appropriation was granted and the Board reported that a lighthouse similar to the one then under construction at Sharp's Island—"an iron caisson 30 feet in diameter and 30 feet high, surmounted by an iron tower 37 feet high"—would be erected at the chosen site.

Beginning in June of 1882, construction proceeded smoothly and, on October 1, 1882, the light was exhibited for the first time. "This light," the Board stated in its 1883 report, "not only marks Bloody Point Bar...but it is a useful Chesapeake Bay light, as a straight run can be made from it to Sandy Point buoy, or the reverse, thus avoiding Thomas's Point Shoal, should that light be destroyed by the ice."

In 1883, one year after the brand new light was commissioned, Bloody Point Bar began to list to the south. Dredging and the construction of a 760-ton scour apron of heavy stone reduced the list from six to two degrees. Photo (c. 1950), Collection P. Hornberger.

By the following year, however, the new tower had tilted. "Severe gales occurred on February 29 and March 3 in this locality," the Board reported, "scouring the sand from under the northwest side of the light-house and causing a settling of the structure toward that direction. The inclination is about 5 feet from the perpendicular at the focal plane." Riprap stone was immediately placed around the northwest side of the caisson, but the stone filling quickly disappeared—either it was scoured away or sank into the soft bottom of the bay. The following year the Board attempted to permanently level and stabilize the lighthouse.

> [S]and was dredged from under a part of the structure until the tower moved in the proper direction. The structure could not be kept in a vertical position, although much care was used, but the inclination is less than one-half as great as before.

After the excavation had been filled, heavy brush mattresses, projecting 30 feet from the structure, were placed entirely around it, and were loaded with small stone. Then, in May 1885, 760 tons of large stone was deposited around the lighthouse to form a scour apron. "It is expected," the Board noted, "that by this means further scour and consequent settlement will be pre-

48

Keith Walters

vented." In fact, their predictions have been largely borne out and the light-house—which at the time correctives were begun had been listing at approximately six degrees—still lists at only two degrees to the south.

In 1960, a terrible fire and explosion caused the lighthouse to be abandoned by the two young coastguardsmen on duty at the time. Engineman Mark L. Mighall and Seaman Haywood H. Savage, aged 19 and 20, fought the blaze as the fire spread from the equipment room just above the water line to their living quarters and then spread rapidly towards a storage room containing drums of fuel and propane gas tanks. "We would use the extinguishers until the smoke got us, then run outside for air," Mighall told *The Baltimore American*. "We did this maybe three or four times until the fire spread into the kitchen and living room." But when the fire "headed for the 500-gallon gas tank," the two young men knew that they had to abandon their station.

In 1960, fire completely destroyed the interior of Bloody Point Bar and almost cost two young coastguardsmen their lives. Today the lighthouse is a hollow cast-iron shell. Photo, U.S. Coast Guard.

Barely succeeding in releasing the manually operated clutch on the automatic boat hoist, their launch was lowered through flames spitting paint and tar to within an inch of the water line as Savage used a twenty-foot oar to hold in the clutch. "It was just touching the water, but not enough to float the boat free from the davits. Neither of us had a knife to cut the block and tackle. We were stuck there—an inch from escape," Mighall said. "I prayed," he continued, "believe me I did." Miraculously, it seemed, the two were freed by a big wave only moments before the explosions occurred.

A U.S. Coast Guard cutter and two utility boats fought the blaze for over 6 hours, but the fire consumed the timber frame interior. Following the fire, the floors and all three stories of the brick masonry lining were removed, exposing the flange connections of the cast-iron plates. In addition, except for the cast-iron brackets supporting the cantilever of the lantern deck, all exterior architectural features were also removed. Now, all that remains is a cast-iron shell and a vertical steel ladder, providing access to the lantern, that is covered to within eight feet of the first level by a protective cage.

A 1948 article, appearing in *The Baltimore Sun*, described the interior of the lighthouse in better days and Tom White's sojourn as lighthouse keeper.*

> *Inside, the lighthouse is made up of five rooms—one below the surface of the water—all with curving walls. The bottom room, reached by a steep metal ladder, is lined with shelves containing paint cans, heavy*

---

*According to White, life on the lighthouse was not very restful. "You cook and scrub and paint and do the wash," he said. "You learn to sleep four hours at a time—which is a little hard sometimes when the horn is sounding off, but you get used to it." According to White, life on Bloody Point Bar was "no place for a man who wants to rest." "When I was first assigned to the light," he said, "I must have worn our five pairs of shoes walking around the decks. I felt trapped—as if there wasn't enough room to move—but that was only for the first few weeks. After that, there was more than enough to do, and I got all the exercise I wanted."

50

ropes and extra pulleys. Two large tanks, each of 250 gallons capacity, are the light's reservoirs; rainwater piped from the roof is stored in them.

The first deck above the water line contains the central controls for the light—the bank of storage batteries that supplies power for the lamp and the other electrical appliances in the building. Nearby are the machinery that operates the foghorn and various lockers containing tools and storm gear.

On the first deck, too, is the room that serves as kitchen, parlor, dining room and radio shack. Here are the stove and refrigerator and heating equipment. Along one side of the wall are two radio sets, one a stand-by and one operating constantly, day and night, bringing the latest information on matters concerning navigation in the bay and rivers.

The article goes on to describe the spiral stairway leading to sparsely furnished sleeping quarters on the second and watch levels, and, finally, the 10-sided cast-iron lantern, where the fourth-order Fresnel lens—capable of magnifying the light from an ordinary 100-watt bulb so that it could be seen for 13 miles—was polished and "given the care lavished on a favorite child." In case of an electric power failure, there was also a supply of kerosene-burning Aladdin's lamps with a range of approximately nine miles. Similarly, the fog horn was backed up by a bell, cast by J. Regester & Sons of Baltimore in 1882, and the motorboat, kept in good running order for emergency rescue work, was backed up by a small dory.

According to the Maryland Historical Trust's 1991 report, the gravitational stability of the structure is fine, but the cast-iron plates exhibit many cracks and the bottom two tiers are severely corroded. In addition, they found that water has entered the interface between the steel cylinder and its concrete filling so that with seasonal temperature changes, especially freezing during the winter months, further deterioration of the caisson structure is inevitable. The cantilevered lantern deck, formed of cast-iron triangular segments and supported by decorative cast-iron brackets, is in good condition. On the south side of the lantern, two solar panels and a battery case have become a favorite osprey nesting site. The original Fresnel lens has been replaced with an acrylic version—its light an incandescent bulb. At low tide, the scour apron is partially visible.

The Maryland Historical Trust has recommended spending a modest sum (approximately $44,000) on the stabilization of the lighthouse shell and caisson substructure. Its potential for other use seems low. Besides continuing to serve as an important navigational aid, the primary interest and value of Bloody Point light will likely be historical—and will need to be presented in conjunction with other nearby lighthouses—at least for the foreseeable future.

Light station established:
1882

Construction of present structure:
1882

Location:
In approximately 8 feet of water on Bloody Point Bar, one and a half miles west of Kent Point, Kent Island, Maryland, at the entrance to the eastern Chesapeake Bay.

Position:
38 50 (05)
76 23 (30)

Characteristic of light:
Active. Flashing white, 6 second intervals; two red sectors, from 003 to 022 degrees, and from 183 to 202 degrees, covering the shoals off Poplar Island.

Height of light, above mean high water:
54 feet.

Range:
White sector, 9 miles; red sector, 7 miles.

Description of station:
Brown tower on brown cylindrical foundation; lantern black.

Fog signal:
One blast every 30 seconds (3-second blast), continuous from September 15 to June 1.

Sharps Island

On the eastern side of the Chesapeake Bay, about four miles from the southern tip of Tilghman Island, the dramatically tilted caisson of the Sharps Island light station marks the shoals off Poplar Island and Black Walnut Point at the entrance to the Choptank River. The present structure was preceded by two other lighthouses, the first of which was constructed on an island of 900 acres, now completely submerged in the bay. During the 17th century, the island had three consecutive owners: William Claiborne, John Bateman and Peter Sharp, a Quaker doctor for whom the island and its lighthouse were named.

By the end of the 19th century the waters of the Chesapeake were advancing on Sharps Island at a rate of over 100 feet per year. Even so, some development of the attractive island continued and a resort hotel was constructed by an ambitious Baltimore boot and shoe manufacturer, Milton R. Creighton. By 1900 only 94 acres of the island remained, and the ill-fated hotel slowly began to disappear—the materials used in its construction quite possibly salvaged by residents of nearby Poplar and Tilghman Islands.

In 1837, Congress paid $600 for ten acres of land on Sharps Island and appropriated $5,000 for construction of the first lighthouse. The fixed light, refitted with a fifth-order lens in 1855, sat on top of a keeper's dwelling, a dwelling deliberately constructed of wood so that it could easily be moved, (by the beginning of the 19th century, erosion of the island was clearly underway). In 1848, when the island had lost approximately half its acreage, the entire lighthouse structure was moved inland. Once again, in 1865, the bay had reached one corner of the building ("leaving no doubt," the Light-House Board reported, "as to the result"). The Board urgently recommended construction of a new lighthouse of screwpile design.

In 1865, even as construction of the new screwpile lighthouse was going on, the urgent necessity of a new light was brought home when for a two-week period no light could be shown at Sharps Island:

[With] the gradual washing away of the ground on which the old light-house at Sharp's Island is built, it became necessary to remove all the furniture from it, including the illuminating apparatus. Hence, from the 1st to the 15th of November, 1865, no light was exhibited from this point. Meanwhile, a tripod of wood-work was constructed, and a steamer's lens established on it which was exhibited on the night of the 16th of December. This temporary appliance will be continued until the new tower now in progress is finished.

In spite of frequent exposure to heavy ice, the screwpile foundation held fast for almost 14 years. But then, given the light's open location near the deepest waters of the bay, the inevitable happened, and in 1881 the Board

Three Sharps Island lighthouses were built: the first, a tower on Sharps Island proper, the second, a screwpile light on the shoals in the vicinity of the island, and the third, the iron caisson tower which remains today. The island, once a prosperous agricultural community, disappeared in the early 20th century. Photo, The National Archives.

Keith Walters

reported that the second lighthouse had been destroyed. "By a heavy run of ice on February 10, this light-house was torn from its foundation and carried away; there was no loss of life; the keepers remained on the wreck until it grounded..." (Incidentally, no report is made of what must have been a harrowing five-mile ride for the keepers through the icy waters of the bay. "[T]heir conduct is highly commended," was the Board's only comment.)

In less than a month's time, Congress had appropriated $35,000 for a third lighthouse and the Light-House Board lost no time in putting this money to use.

> *Deeming an ordinary screw-pile light-house at this place liable to be again destroyed by the heavy runs of ice so prevalent in Chesapeake Bay in severe winters, it was determined to use a cast-iron caisson filled with concrete and surmounted by a tower, also of cast iron, with a brick lining. The solidity and great weight of such a structure it is thought will be effective.*

In spite of construction delays, the 37-foot iron tower, resting on an iron caisson 30 feet in diameter and 30 feet in height, was nearing completion by early winter, 1882, and though the dwelling lacked water cisterns to collect rain water and other amenities, the ever-hardy keepers moved in and the fixed-white, fourth-order lens, manufactured by the French firm of Barbier and Fenestre in 1881, was exhibited on February 1, 1882.

The open-water location of the Sharps Island light has always been subject to scour and to heavy ice floes, and during several severe Chesapeake winters in the 1970's—especially in 1976 and 1977—the Sharps Island lighthouse was tilted by the impact of extremely heavy moving ice. The new—and unusual—inclination of the lighthouse tower necessitated the removal of the fourth-order lens and its replacement with a 250 mm. plastic lens which was placed on a leveling plate secured to the original light pedestal.

The present condition of both the exterior and interior of the tower is extremely poor and has been described in detail by the Maryland Historical Trust. Listing at 15 degrees, the caisson's iron plates now exhibit cracks caused by freeze and thaw at the iron and concrete interface of the caisson cylinder as well as corrosion due to lack of paint. Window sashes have been largely removed, though the unusual decorative cast-iron heads remain at the windows on the third level. The concrete deck of the six-foot-wide gallery at the first level, once covered with a roof, is crumbling, permitting water penetration into the substructure, and an open door, unglazed windows, and an uncovered coal chute have allowed water to wash into the first level, rotting the wooden floor and causing further deterioration of its concrete substratum as well as spalling of the brick masonry lining.

Ascending the interior wooden stairway which follows the curve of the caisson wall, the second, third, and watch levels of the tower show damage caused by a combination of exposure to the elements and poor ventilation—especially at the watch level where seven equally spaced porthole windows have been glazed with non-ventilated acrylic. Additionally, the exterior cast-iron plates exhibit cracks and some of them are loose. The floors are constructed of radial segments of cast iron bolted together with the flanges turned upwards to create a smooth ceiling below. The floors are finished in wood and are in poor condition.

The 10-sided cast-iron lantern rises from a cantilevered deck supported by brackets and constructed, as are the interior floors, of radial cast-iron segments (though here the flanges are turned downward to create a smooth deck surface). One of the radial segments is cracked.

The estimated cost of repair and stabilization of the Sharps Island light is high (at this writing, over a quarter of a million dollars) and there have been intimations that the Coast Guard will abandon the structure. If abandoned, the lighthouse will be turned over to the General Services Administration who will first make it available to federal, state, and local governments, and then, if no interest is expressed on the part of these agencies, to private bidders. Sadly, like Bloody Point light, the Sharps Island light is relatively inaccessible and would appear to have no immediate reuse value (unlike the ill-fated hotel built on Sharps Island at the turn of the century) —at least not in its present location—unless it is incorporated into educational programs on Chesapeake Bay history and tours that would link it to other lighthouses on the bay.

The continuing deterioration faced by Sharps Island light if it remains in its present location offers a good illustration of the relative merits of leaving historical structures in place versus moving them for preservation purposes. At least one eastern-shore town has expressed an interest in acquiring the light and has offered to restore it and to provide historical displays and interpretations that would be readily accessible to the public. Purists, however, argue that once the lighthouse is removed from its original location, its historical significance will be lost. (Perhaps there is much truth to this, but if destruction of the historical structure is the inevitable result of inaction, is it still a useful point?) Boaters, too, find that the presence of familiar and distinctive lighthouses offer them more reliable assistance in navigation than skeletal towers do—especially as day marks. Sooner or later, these questions will probably be debated for other lighthouses in the deeper channels of the bay. Meanwhile, it is extremely difficult to obtain permission to move a lighthouse (even when this means that it is extremely difficult to save a lighthouse), especially in Maryland, where state law now specifically forbids their relocation. Sharps Island light may offer the first challenge to the rigidness of that law.

Cove Point

At the request of the Fifth Auditor of the Treasury an appropriation for a lighthouse to mark the entrance to the Patuxent River at Cedar Point was made by Congress on March 3, 1825. For many years, mariners and shipping interests had been pointing to the need for a lighthouse that would serve both north and southbound vessels in the Chesapeake Bay as well as one that would guide southbound vessels entering the Patuxent River. Thus, it was decided that Cove Point, four miles north of the entrance to the Patuxent, offered a superior site and three years later, on February 12, 1828, a new appropriation of $5,685 was made for a lighthouse at the new location. Four and one-half acres at Cove Point

were purchased from Dorcas G. Bourne on June 12, 1828 for the sum of $300, and within two months John Donahoo had been awarded a contract for construction of the lighthouse and work on the tower and detached white dwelling was begun.

Both the tower—just over 38 feet from base to lantern deck—and the keeper's dwelling were built of locally manufactured brick. The tower, painted white, is in the shape of a truncated cone, its masonry now covered with stucco. The circular lantern, with cast-iron mullions supported by a masonry wall and surrounded by an 18-inch stone deck and cast-iron railing, has triangular panes of glass and is painted black. The interior floor of the lantern is formed of a single iron plate.

The interior winding staircase is unusually attractive. It is constructed of wooden treads, triangular in shape with a hole on the interior side through which a central wooden column is threaded. The outside (or outboard) of each tread is fitted directly into the masonry of the tower as is a narrow handrail which appears to be original. Standing on the ground floor one looks up at a spiral of beautiful symmetry winding around the central pole. Next to the stairwell column a square shaft, also running from the ground level to the lantern, houses the counterweights of the original winding mechanism.

During daylight hours, French-cut crystal lenses were carefully protected with linen dust covers. Cove Point was originally outfitted with a fifth-order Fresnel lens, but it was replaced with this fourth-order lens in 1899. Photo, The Mariners' Museum, Newport News.

The entranceway faces west and the door, a replacement of the original, apparently had to be installed upside down because, at the time it was constructed, the ventilation louver was improperly placed at the top of the door. Ascending the tower are three small windows, the lowest of the three facing to the north. At the base of the tower, the walls are over 30 inches thick.

The Cove Point light, first exhibited in December 1828, used 11 lamps with a like number of 18-inch reflectors. James Somerville was selected from seven applicants and appointed its first keeper in December of 1828 at an annual salary of $350. The "old reflecting apparatus" was replaced in June of 1855 with a fifth-order Fresnel lens. In 1899, electric lamps were first installed (though the light was not fully electrified until 1907), and, also in 1899, the fifth-order Fresnel lens

The light tower, built in 1828, is close to the water's edge and erosion of the lighthouse site has been the major upkeep problem, necessitating the construction of a sea wall as early as 1892. Photo (c. 1930), U.S. Coast Guard.

August Selckmann

was in turn replaced by a more powerful, "new-model" fourth-order lens. This lens, manufactured in Paris in 1897 (one can see the manufacturer's original engraving plate on the base of the lens) is still used in the lighthouse and rests on top of a brass and glass box which, though no longer is use, houses the winding mechanism which at one time rotated the light creating the flashing effect. Today, although an electric motor has supplanted the gear works and counterweights of this late 19th century winding mechanism, its parts are still connected and fully operational. The pristine condition of both the winding mechanism and Fresnel lens are a reminder that the presence of personnel at a light station, even one that is fully automated, is a powerful deterrent to the kind of vandalism that has wrought irreparable damage to other Chesapeake Bay lighthouses—for example, Turkey Point and Sandy Point where irreplaceable Fresnel lenses have been lost.

The Cove Point station was first outfitted with a fog bell in 1834. This fog-bell house was built in 1901 for a blower siren and machinery. The iron bell was kept on the roof for use in emergencies. Photo, U.S. Coast Guard.

The 34-by-20-foot stone dwelling, painted white, followed the same floor plan that Donahoo used in his other Chesapeake lighthouses and was similar to other keeper's homes of the early 19th century. In 1883, the house was enlarged by the addition of a second story (as were all the diminutive keeper's quarters designed by Donahoo). "The roof of the dwelling was removed in May, the walls were raised, and a new roof, covered with tin, was constructed," the annual report of the Light House Board stated. "The three rooms were plastered and finished, and other repairs were made to the dwelling and tower. With the enlargement, the station has six good rooms and a good basement or cellar, and is in excellent order." In 1953, the entire lighthouse, but not the keeper's dwelling, was surfaced with cement.

Money for a fog bell was likewise appropriated twice, first in 1834, and, again, in 1837. According to the annual reports of 1858, 1868, 1869, 1880, 1881 and 1887, the fog bell machinery and frame (unlike the tower and dwelling), frequently required major overhaul or replacement. In 1892, when it was noted that "[t]he foundation of the fog-bell tower...had already been reached by the water line," it was moved 16 feet inland. Then, in 1898, the Board announced that "an iron fog-bell tower" had been erected during the month of December 1897 "to replace a dilapidated wooden one" (actually the one built only a few years before). "The new tower," the report continued optimistically, "is a square pyramidal skeleton structure, 31 feet high, standing on and anchored to brick piers 3 feet by 3 feet in plan. ... On February 4, 1898, a test was made of the audibility of the fog signal, with satisfactory results."

58

Nevertheless, by 1901 yet another replacement was called for—this time by improved technology. "In April," the annual report stated, "the iron bell tower was removed, and in May a structure, 12 feet by 16 feet in plan, with brick foundation walls and a wooden frame and sheathing, was erected on the site for housing a blower siren and machinery. A support was provided on the roof for the fog bell, for use in emergencies." Finally, in 1976, the air-powered horn was replaced with an electric diaphone signal which can be heard at a distance of two miles from the station.

Over the years the sturdy brickwork of Donahoo's lighthouse and keeper's dwelling required much re-cementing, plastering, painting, whitewashing and re-roofing, but with this steady maintenance the structures have remained essentially sound for well over 150 years. The encroaching waters of the Chesapeake and consequent erosion of the lighthouse site have always been of major concern at Cove Point. In 1892, the first sea wall was constructed to halt rapid erosion of the lighthouse property and intrusion on the tower. It was, the Board reported, "composed of 4-inch sheet piling, 12 feet long, forced into the ground and backed by 6-inch waling pieces, bolted to heavy piles, 25 feet long, driven 12 feet apart on a line 340 feet long."

During the 1970's there was talk of decommissioning the light and the Calvert Marine Museum made a bid to acquire the property which had been listed on the Calvert County Historic Inventory in 1972 and on the National Register of Historic Places in 1973. Nothing came of these plans, however, and the three coastguardsmen assigned to the station remained until March 1986, when orders for the complete automation of Cove Point arrived by mail. On August 16, 1986, the conversion was officially completed. New electronic equipment included a fog detector that would automatically activate the fog horn when visibility dropped below three miles, an automatic lampchanger, and a computer, connected to Baltimore headquarters, that monitors all these controls. (One can't help but wonder: What would John Donahoo think about the operation of his lighthouse today?)

The Cove Point light station, according to the Maryland Historical Trust, has an excellent reuse potential. Besides being adjacent to attractive fossil-strewn beaches, the site has several buildings suitable for conversion to a small inn. Its location is along one of Maryland's most active "tourist corridors." In recent years, the Coast Guard has erected a fence around the property because a steady stream of tourists and visitors wandered around the former keeper's dwellings and other outbuildings, often requesting impromptu tours of the lighthouse. These houses are now used as private residences for Coast Guard personnel and their families attached to St. Inigoes. Presently, weekend tours are available from Memorial Day through the end of October. Overall, the lighthouse is in excellent condition and a point of pride for the U.S. Coast Guard.

Light station established:
1828

Construction of present structure:
1828

Location:
Four miles north entrance to the Patuxent River, west side of the Chesapeake Bay, Maryland.

Position:
38 23 10
76 22 55

Characteristic of light:
Flashing white, 10 second intervals.

Height of light, above mean high water:
45 feet.

Range:
19 miles.

Description of station:
Detached white masonry tower, black lantern; white keeper's dwelling, second residence and other outbuildings, all painted white.

Fog signal:
Horn: 1 blast every 15 seconds (2-second blast). Cove Point Radiobeacon: CP (-.-. .—.); frequency: 314 kHz; antenna 60 feet at 175 degrees from Cove Point light.

Drum Point

In an abbreviated report dated July 21, 1856, 5th Lighthouse District inspector W. H. Murdough briefly sketched out plans for a lighthouse at Drum Point to mark the shoals by the north side of the entrance to the Patuxent River—a spot where several ships had run aground. "Structure to be placed on the extreme south point of land. Focal plane to be elevated 25 feet above the horizon. Apparatus of the 6th Order—illuminating an arc of 270 degrees, showing a fixed light." Just over two weeks later, the 5th District's top engineer likewise reported:

> On the 24th inst. at 5 a.m., I took the apparatus on Shore and commenced boring at the Point selected, and penetrated to a depth of 13$^1/_2$ feet through very hard sand. We exerted the full power of 4 men with 175 lbs. on the auger. I think it will require spur wheel gearing to drive 3-feet Screws 8 or 9 feet deep, which there is no doubt, will be perfectly safe for the structure proposed at this place, being on the shore. The operations at this point was perfectly satisfactory, the soil being clean sand to the depth penetrated.

Notwithstanding an act of the Maryland legislature, approved on March 3, 1853, ceding jurisdiction over the site, and an appropriation of $5,000 authorized by Congress on August 3, 1854, the Board reported in 1857 that clear title to the site had not yet been obtained. In fact, the proposed construction was dropped for almost 30 years until Congress once again appropriated funds, this time $25,000—a sum actually meant to fund construction of two range lights. In the end, however, the Light-House Board decided against the range lights and erected a screwpile lighthouse instead—the last screwpile lighthouse built on the Chesapeake Bay to survive to the present day, albeit in a museum setting.*

> The smallness of the appropriation, as well as the absence of necessity for a range here, caused the Board to erect a screw-pile light-house at Drum Point, which answers the present requirements of commerce. ... The structure, like those at Hooper's Straits and Jane's Island, is an hexagonal frame building upon seven wrought-iron 10-inch piles, securely tied and braced.

At the time it was built, Drum Point light stood in approximately ten feet of water and sailing vessels often passed between it and the shore. At the turn of the century, however, the light stood in only about three feet of water and by the late 1970's, when the light was moved to the Calvert Marine Museum, it was completely landlocked. The fixed red light, exhibited for the first time

Drum Point light was home to many keepers and their families. Here, William Yeatman poses with his children. Notice that silting has already apparently begun to bring the lighthouse closer to the shore. Photo, Calvert Marine Museum.

---

*The following screwpile lights—all of them now gone—were constructed after Drum Point light: Craney Island light on the Elizabeth River, 1884; Great Shoals on the Wicomico River in Maryland, 1884; Old Plantation Flats in Virginia, 1886; Great Wicomico River light, in Virginia, 1889; Cobb Point Bar on the north side of the Potomac, 1889; Tangier Sound in Virginia on the eastern side of the bay, 1890; Greenbury Point Shoal, on the north side of the entrance to Annapolis, 1891; Maryland Point, also on the Potomac, 1892; Sharkfin Shoal northeast of Bloodsworth Island, 1892; and Pages Rock on the York River, 1893.

August Selckmann

on August 20, 1883, was housed in a fourth-order Fresnel lens manufactured in France; its prisms had an arc of only 270 degrees (since the remaining 90 degrees of the arc showed over land). Later the light was changed to contain only three red sectors. The focal plane of the light was 45^1/$_2$ feet above mean high water and was visible over 11 nautical miles. (The original lens—in pristine condition—is once again in the lantern at the Calvert Marine Museum resting on the original cast-iron pedestal.)

Drum Point light is a one-and-a-half-story cottage, balloon-framed over a steel frame and covered with molded clapboard siding. The cottage is painted white with a rich sienna-red roof and piles. Two doors and six double-hung windows open out onto the main gallery and two dormer windows project from the standing seam metal roof. The gallery deck has rounded wooden posts and square balustrades with a circular handrail (now restored). A privy is cantilevered from the main deck. Inside the first level are a sitting room, keeper's bedroom, dining room and kitchen. A circular stairway winding around a central wooden column leads to the second level accommodating an additional bedroom and the bell room. Yet another winding stairway leads to the lantern. The octagonal lantern is constructed of wood clad in metal and painted black. The storm-panel frames are cast iron, the lantern roof is pyramidal, topped with a ventilator ball. The balustrade of the lantern gallery matches that of the main deck.

Most of the building parts were prefabricated and shipped to the site. Thus, actual construction of the attractive cottage lighthouse was completed in just over a month. In April, 1883, Allentown Rolling Mills of Philadelphia signed a contract to furnish the metal-work—ten-inch diameter wrought-iron piles fitted with three-foot-wide auger flanges which were bored into the hard sand substratum of the Patuxent River. Work crews began construction on July 17, 1883, and, according to the Light-House Board, "on the 24th the ironwork was in position and the setting up of the wooden superstructure begun. By the middle of August the house was finished, with the exception of some painting, which a small force was left to complete."

In its new location over Backwater Creek, Drum Point light retains some of the visual sensibility of its original shallow water location. Photo, Calvert Marine Museum.

The 1400-pound fog bell, struck by a 30-pound bell hammer attached to 600-pound weights, sounded a double blow every 15 seconds. The weights were wound every two hours by the keeper during times of low visibility. The bell was cast by the McShane Bell Foundry of Baltimore in 1880.

Unlike many of the screwpile lighthouses of the Chesapeake Bay and its tributaries, Drum Point weathered ice and storms and generally required only minor repairs. The worst damage occurred in the summer of 1933 when a violent storm flooded the cottage and lodged a large tree against the pilings. The lighthouse motorboat was sunk, the skiff was cast adrift, and the rain gauge and weather instruments were washed away. The keeper, surveying his options, matter-of-factly concluded a letter requesting assistance with the observation that the only means of getting ashore was to swim. And apparently, letter in hand, he did.

In 1944 the station was electrified though, during the Second World War, it was often darkened. (During training maneuvers on the Chesapeake Bay, keeper John Hansen recalled that the Army or Navy would call him on the radio and tell him to put out the light.) In 1960 the beacon was automated and in 1962 service was discontinued. From that time until 1975, when the lighthouse was taken over by the Calvert County Historical Society to become part of the Calvert Marine Museum two miles away, vandalism, neglect and bureaucratic red tape caused almost irreversible damage to the abandoned structure. Nature, too, had a hand in this, for silting pushed the shoreline into the bay, eventually placing the lighthouse solidly on dry land where it was easily accessible to vandals. Meanwhile, former lighthouse keepers and interested citizens stood helplessly by. "Often at night," former keeper John

Hansen remarked, "I dream of restoring the lighthouse. I see things that need to be fixed up, painted. I go looking for tools and supplies, but find nothing."

In 1966, the Calvert County Historical Society decided to adopt the lighthouse as a restoration project and took steps to acquire the lighthouse property. But the group soon discovered that political skirmishing, not to mention the imponderable machinations of local, state and federal government agencies with regard to the lighthouse and the site, posed formidable obstacles to the realization of their plans.

Meanwhile, the condition of the lighthouse deteriorated. By 1973, when the society succeeded in having the Drum Point light placed on the National Register of Historic Places, the entire structure had been repeatedly vandalized—twenty-two doors and twelve windows were broken and the interior was defaced with graffiti. In addition, parts of the building had been set on fire (more than once), attempts had been made to steal the fog bell (which because of its high silver content had to be removed for safekeeping), and the railings around the gallery and widow's walk had been ripped out. Meanwhile, efforts to acquire the lighthouse continued and, finally, in 1974, the society was told that it could have the lighthouse proper but not any part of the site. Shortly thereafter, with the help of the Calvert County government and a $25,000 grant from the state of Maryland, title was transferred and arrangements were made to move the lighthouse to the Calvert Marine Museum.

The actual move took two days and was carried out in March of 1975 by the B.F. Diamond Construction Company of Savannah, Georgia (then at work on construction of the Thomas Johnson bridge in nearby Solomons). They generously agreed to move the lighthouse for the funds that the state grant had provided. A powerful tugboat towed the barge with a steam-operated crane and 110-foot boom to Drum Point where workmen began their efforts to cut the seven wrought-iron screw pilings which supported the structure. To their amazement, they found the 10-inch-diameter iron pilings to be solid metal—meaning, not only that the cutting operation required an extra day, but also that the weight of the structure had been greatly underestimated. Nevertheless, the crew continued working into the night until foul weather and fatigue forced them to suspend their efforts. As soon as the weather improved, the work crews returned. A tackle was fitted to the metal foundation pilings and, with great clanging and with steam billowing from the crane, the actual hoisting began. Two tugboats gingerly pulled the barge and crane, now dangling a 41-ton lighthouse, up the Patuxent River to its brand-new foundation on a pier extending out over Backwater Creek next to the Calvert Marine Museum.

With donations from the National Park Service and the Maryland Historical Trust, not to mention private donations and the assistance of former keepers and their families, the Drum Point light has been restored to mint condition and furnished much as it was at the turn of the century. It's future, as part of a growing regional history museum and nature study center, seems assured.

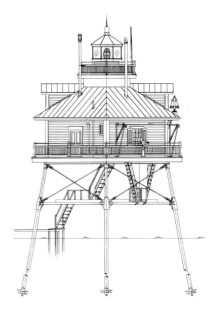

Light station established:
1883

Construction of present structure:
1883

Location:
Calvert Marine Museum, Solomons, Maryland.

Characteristic of light:
Inactive, but original lens and light are on display in the lighthouse.

Description of station:
White hexagonal cottage on cast-iron pilings.

Hooper Island

As evident by its shape and color, the architectural style of Hooper Island light is often referred to as "spark plug". Photo (c. 1902) National Archives.

Hooper Island light is one of five lighthouses built on the Chesapeake Bay during the 20th century; Baltimore Light, Point No Point, Thimble Shoal and Chesapeake light (constructed much later and technically a sea coast light) are the other four. Together with Baltimore Light and Point No Point, Hooper Island Light represents the end of an era—an era in which the lighthouse keeper and lighthouse were still thought of as inseparable—and the beginning of a century which would end with the automation of lighthouses throughout the United States and the complete obsolescence of the job of lighthouse keeper. In 1897, however, when the Light-House Board requested funds for a light to be situated between Cove Point and Smith Point, pride and excitement were still centered on the technological and engineering feasibility of constructing sturdy lighthouses in parts of the bay formerly considered off limits.

Hooper Island light is situated in 18 feet of water on the west end of the shoal making off from Hooper Island on the east side of the Chesapeake Bay. It was designed to protect mariners from the "dreaded" shoals along the eastern side of the bay—a lonely 30-mile stretch between Smith Point and Cove Point known to be treacherous for ships of deep draft heading towards Baltimore and the upper bay. In 1898 Congress appropriated funds for the light and the following year a contract was awarded. The caisson was to be sunk using the pneumatic process (apparently only 11 lighthouses were constructed in the United States using this method of sinking the foundation) and the engineering difficulties which its construction presented are brought home by the fact that the first contracting company failed even to begin the work. Bids were reopened and a second contract was awarded in 1900 when work on the light station began in earnest and proceeded—unlike the fiasco surrounding construction of Baltimore Light—in a relatively uneventful fashion.

On July 6, 1901, the caisson was in position and, by the end of August, the caisson had been sunk to the required depth of 13 and one-half feet beneath the muddy bottom of the bay. Work was finished in the spring of 1902 and the flashing white light in a fourth-order Fresnel lens, manufactured by F. Barbier & Company in Paris in 1888, was first exhibited on the tower. The focal plane of the light is 63 feet. Constructed of brick and iron, the lighthouse caisson is painted brown, the tower is painted white, and the watch level and lantern, with a round cast-iron roof, copper ventilator ball, and the mullions of the diamond-shaped storm panels are painted black. The interior of the tower was also white except for the cast-iron stair treads which were painted brown. In 1904, the characteristic of the light was changed to fixed white varied by a flash every 15 seconds. Later on it was changed back to flashing white on a 10-second cycle (flash one second, eclipse two seconds, flash one second, eclipse six seconds). Initially, the 44-and-one-half inch diameter fog bell, manufactured by McShane of Baltimore in 1901, was kept as

Starke Jett

a backup for a Cunningham air diaphragm foghorn after a generator system was installed in the late 1930's. Today the foghorn is powered by solar panels.

Hooper Island light was changed to full automatic operation on November 21, 1961. Fifteen years later the costly and irreplaceable Fresnel lens was stolen and a modern marine lamp was installed in its stead.

Although only 18 feet of the caisson is visible above mean high water, the caisson stands 36 feet above the bottom of the bay. Except for boarding hatchways on the eastern and western sides of the caisson, the top tier of iron plates flare out to support the gallery deck. According to the Maryland Historical Trust, the original cast-iron deck and gallery roof have been removed and the deck replaced with carelessly laid concrete affording poor drainage. In places, the coarse-aggregate concrete filling is exposed to the elements and along the rim of the deck, moisture is able to penetrate the iron and concrete interface of the caisson foundation. They recommend that the roof and deck be replaced with rolled iron plate to prevent further moisture damage. The exterior caisson also shows more cracking than any of the lights included in the Maryland Historical Trust's study and these cracks need to be filled with sealant.

The tower is a truncated cone consisting of five tiers of cast-iron plates—generally in good condition—with the flanges bolted on the inside creating a smooth exterior surface. The tower's ten windows are decorated with cast-iron pediments, also in good condition. The tower is lined with brick, glazed white on one side to provide a smooth interior finish. In addition to the lantern, the tower contains four levels, a watch level, and a lower level where the brick and concrete cisterns once stored water drained from the gallery roof. A 13-inch diameter, load-bearing hollow iron column extending from the lower level to the lantern deck also provided a free fall for the winding mechanism's counterweights.

From the first level, which once served as the kitchen, a curved iron-tread stairway bolted to the iron plates of the exterior wall leads to the second, third and fourth levels which afforded sleeping, storage and living space to the keepers. The fourth level has five porthole windows and a curved iron ship's ladder that provides access through a hatchway into the watch level. All the floors are wooden—and in various states of repair—except the watch level and lantern level which are diamond cast-iron plate. Both levels have cantilevered gallery decks—the watch level deck is supported by decorative iron brackets.

In general, Hooper Island light remains in good condition. It is still an active navigational aid maintained by the U.S. Coast Guard, but because of its remoteness and marine location, its future as an historical structure is uncertain.

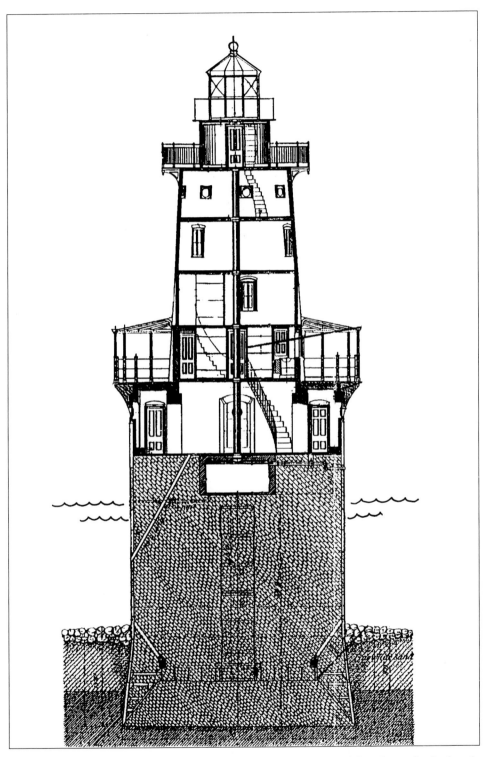

The interior of the Hooper Island tower was lined in white-glazed brick and contained a fourth watch level right below the lantern in addition to three levels for storage, office and living space. The trumpet flare of the last course of caisson plates created a larger gallery deck and a large cellar and storage area which had small porthole windows. Iron caisson towers had fewer decorative flourishes but the greater height of the Hooper Island tower and the diamond pattern of the lantern panes give the lighthouse a pleasing symmetry. Drawing, Gredell & Associates.

Point No Point

Like Baltimore Light, the construction of Point No Point was plagued with difficulties. When a construction pier collapsed, the caisson broke and drifted 40 miles to the south. Several months later, a new construction pier, workmen's quarters and much of the dredging equipment were carried away by heavy ice floes. The light was finally commissioned in 1905. Photo, U.S. Coast Guard.

Although the lighthouse at Point No Point, two miles off the western bay shore of St. Mary's County (approximately six miles north of Point Lookout and nine miles south by southwest of Hooper Island light), was not commissioned until April of 1905, the first request for an appropriation from the Light-House Board came in 1891. In its recommendation, the Light-House·Board took note of two problems—the first, dangerous shoals extending out from the western shore of the bay, and the second, a 30-mile stretch of water between Smith Point and Cove Point that was inadequately lighted. "For a part of the distance," the Board wrote, "navigators are without a guide, where a deviation from their sailing course might carry vessels of heavy draught onto dangerous shoals." In their estimation, the increase of such large craft on the bay made the construction of a light station highly desirable. An appropriation of $35,000 was asked for, but to no avail, and, thus, the recommendation, essentially unchanged except for an increasing price tag, was repeated throughout the 1890's. In 1899, the Board noted in its annual report that "petitions for a light at this locality have lately become quite urgent," and asked for $65,000 to complete the light station.

Finally, in March of 1901, the $65,000 appropriation was granted and, shortly thereafter, borings were made at the site and the design of the lighthouse was completed, though it would be more than four years before completion of the lighthouse.

The following year a contract for the construction was awarded to Toomey Brothers of New York and most of the iron superstructure was finished. "Seven sections, or courses, of the foundation cylinder were completed," the Board reported,

> *and three sections were delivered at the Lazaretto light-house depot. Nine plates of the eighth course are out of the sand; the center columns and sockets were fitted together; the covers and frames for the coal and manholes were finished, and the main and lantern gallery railings and the ladders and platforms were turned over to the contractors for erection...*

Work on the caisson had not yet begun, though a construction pier had been built at the site of the lighthouse.

In August of 1902, construction work on the wooden caisson began in earnest and proceeded apace until the end of January. "The balance of the deck was finished," the Board noted, "two courses of iron were set up, and the bulkheads were raised 8 feet high..." Work was resumed on March 24 and on April 3 the caisson was towed to the site. "Soon after," the Board continued,

> *an accident occurred in which the temporary pier built by the contractors during the previous season gave way and the caisson was wrecked. The latter turned over, and after breaking off the second and third courses of cylinder plates, drifted down the bay before a northwest gale.*

Greg Pease

69

Light station established:
1905

Construction of present structure:
1905

Location:
In 22 feet of water, on the point of the shoal making off from Point No Point, six miles north of Point Lookout lighthouse and the mouth of the Potomac River.

Position:
38 07 41
76 17 26

Characteristic of light:
Flashing white, 6-second interval.

Height of light, above mean high water:
52 feet.

Range:
9 miles.

Description of station:
Brown cylindrical foundation pier, expanding in trumpet shape at its upper end, surmounted by a white two-story octagonal brick dwelling with mansard roof; black lantern.

Fog signal:
Horn: 1 blast every 30 seconds (3-second blast), operated continuously from September 15 to June 1.

The contractor's tug followed the caisson and on April 5 it was picked up off the Rappahannock River, 40 miles south of the construction site. With the wrecked caisson anchored off Solomons, Maryland, work began again at the end of June to prepare the caisson for the next attempt to place it at the site. "With a draft of 19 feet and 4 inches," the Board reported, "it was towed from Solomons on the night of October 21, 1903, and was grounded at the site in its correct position on the next afternoon. On October 23, about 225 tons of riprap stone was deposited around it to prevent scour."

With the caisson safely at the site, things were beginning to look up for the contractors. They rebuilt their construction pier and workmen's quarters, finished placing the fifth course of cylinder plates in position, and had filled the cylinder with concrete to within 3 feet of the last course of plates when in early February, as reported by the Board, "the pier was carried away by a heavy field of moving ice, together with the air compressor, the boiler, a section of the air shaft, four cylinder plates, the workmen's quarters, some cement, broken stone, sand, and small tools." Only the boiler and two of the cylinder plates were recovered, but fortunately the caisson suffered little damage. In March, the contractors had to begin construction of yet a third pier while, intermittently, they continued to fill the cylinder with concrete. The pier was completed in May. "They commenced sinking the caisson on June 2," the Board continued. "By the end of June the structure had penetrated 13 feet and the surface of the concrete was 9 inches below the top of the fifth course of cylinder plates..." New cylinder plates had been ordered by the contractors—also for the third time—to replace those lost when the pier was carried away by ice. One can only guess that the contractor, by now, must have felt that Point No Point was an apt name for the lighthouse.

Happily, however, in 1905, the Light-House Board was able to report completion of the Point No Point light station, in spite of delays caused by icy conditions in the bay and its tributaries. "The new structure," the Board reported proudly, "may be described as follows:"

The lower part consists of a wooden caisson, 32 feet square and 13 feet high, which was provided with a working chamber and air shaft for carrying on the operation of sinking the structure by the pneumatic process. These spaces were subsequently filled with concrete. On the roof of the caisson rests a cast-iron foundation cylinder, 30 feet in diameter and 51 feet in height, expanding near the top, which is 18 feet above the water, into a trumpet shape. This cylinder is mainly filled with concrete, spaces being left for a cellar and two cisterns. Surmounting the foundation cylinder is an octagonal brick dwelling, 2 stories high, with a mansard roof, supporting a lantern deck with railing and an 8-sided lantern. A gallery surrounds the house, accessible from the water by means of two sets of ladders, and on it are placed steel davits, boat-hoisting apparatus, and the like. The new light was shown for the first time on April 24, 1905. It is of the fourth order, illuminating the entire horizon, and flashing white and red, alternately, at intervals of 20 seconds. A bell is struck by machinery a double blow every 15 seconds during thick or foggy weather.

Point No Point, situated at the entrance to St. Jerome's Creek in a relatively undeveloped part of St. Mary's County, marks the main north-south ship channel of the Chesapeake Bay and a turning point for southbound ships heading into the Potomac River. Its focal plane is 52 feet above mean high tide. Fully automated since 1938, it has been unmanned since April of 1962. One month before the station was changed to unmanned operation, *Baltimore Sun* writer Philip Evans and photographer A. Aubrey Bodine visited the station. They found an immaculate lighthouse station cared for by three coast-guardsmen who prided themselves on their cooking ("We have a cook book and a whole drawer full of recipes," one said. "Our pineapple upside down cake is real good.") and who were happy to receive company. "[Their] ancient and omnipresent aluminum coffee pot glistens like the commandant's sterling service," Evans wrote. At the time, only three other Chesapeake light stations were manned: the Craighill Channel front light, Sandy Point, and Thomas Point Shoal. Unfortunately, however, in the years since 1962, the interior of the Point No Point dwelling has deteriorated markedly.

The lighthouse is a regular octagon with 11-foot long sides, and, much like Sandy Point, the wood-framed third, or watch level, slopes to the lantern deck forming an attractive octagonal mansard roof, painted black, with four gabled dormer windows. Two courses of corbeled brick above the first-level windows and four above the second add an attractive decorative feature to the masonry stories. The first two masonry levels are painted white; the caisson is brown.

In 1988 and 1989, the Coast Guard made numerous repairs to the lighthouse—the caisson was sandblasted and painted, the roof and cupola were repaired, and the deck railing and access ladders were repaired. Again in 1990 and 1991, the structure was painted and superficially cleaned up, but the interior has continued to decline.

The Maryland Historical Trust reports that the flooring of the first level has been coated with cement and that the second-level flooring and walls (originally the keepers' sleeping quarters) have rotted from extensive water damage and recommends their replacement. Moisture penetration has also caused spalling of some of the brick masonry, though recent painting has halted deterioration of the brick. The heads and sills of all the windows are unpainted pink granite in good condition. The caisson itself is sound.

The black eight-sided lantern is wood-framed with cast-iron mullions for the storm panels. An acrylic lens has replaced the fourth-order Fresnel lens and now rests on the original pedestal. In 1991, the Maryland Historical Trust found the beaded board lining the lantern unpainted and the iron mullions supporting the storm panels both unpainted and badly corroded. In recent years, the original fog bell, still visible in A. Aubrey Bodine's 1962 photographs for *The Baltimore Sun*, has been removed.

Also frequently visible in photographs is the cast-iron privy of irregular hexagonal shape which is cantilevered from the first-level gallery deck. It remains in good condition, sporting a decorative finial on the peak of its pyramidal roof.

Solomons Lump

The first lighthouse located on the shoal known as Solomon's Lump, lit in 1875, was of screwpile design. As early as 1872, the annual report of the Light-House Board suggested that the construction of a new lighthouse to mark the Kedge's Strait shoals, between Tangier Sound and the Chesapeake Bay, would provide safer passage for ships and would allow the Fog Point lighthouse, established in 1827, to be discontinued. "Solomon's Lump," the report stated,

Solomons Lump was changed to unwatched operation in 1950 and the dwelling was soon demolished by the Coast Guard. Photo (1950), U.S. Coast Guard.

> *is a point of land on the north end of Evans Island. There is a shoal that extends out a considerable distance from this point in a northerly direction, and is a source of danger to vessels navigating Kedges Strait at night. Near its extreme point is the regular channel. The shoal itself has not more than about 5 feet water on it to a point near the red buoy, which marks its extreme northerly end. At night this buoy cannot be seen a sufficient distance to be of any use. The only light in this vicinity is that on Fog Point, about one and one-fourth miles in a west-southwest direction, but, on account of its distance and location, it affords no security to vessels from going ashore on the reef off Solomon's Lump. The light at Fog Point was established in 1827, before the introduction of the screw-pile system of light-houses, and though it has served to mark the entrance to Kedges Strait for a long time, it is of little value as compared with other positions that could have been selected for a screw-pile structure, which would not only have marked the entrance to the strait, but would have been a guide all the way through. A light established on the shoal off Solomon's Lump, near its extreme point, and in 5 feet of water, or on the shoal on the opposite side of the channel would accomplish both these objects, and render navigation through Kedges Strait safe at all times. As the sailing course in either direction would be a straight line passing just north of the light-house at Solomon's Lump, in case a light was established there, that at Fog Point would be no longer of use, and could be discontinued. It would, therefore, not increase the number of lights, nor add anything to the annual cost of maintenance.*

The Board requested an appropriation of $15,000, and repeated the request the following year. In 1874, the appropriation was granted and the Light-House Board reported that its construction would be undertaken "without unnecessary delay."

Work on the first lighthouse was begun on June 21, 1875. "The structure will be a screw-pile light-house, on five wrought-iron piles, square in plan, with a lantern surmounting the keeper's dwelling. It is expected that the light will be exhibited during the present season," the Board reported.

Eighteen years later, in late January of 1893, a mass of moving ice proved its destruction. "Though not carried from its site," the Board reported in June of that same year, "the house was pushed over so that part of it is submerged. All the movable property was taken away and stored. In June a lens-lantern light was established on the wreck to mark its position at night and afford assistance to local navigation."

Starke Jett

Light station established:
1875

**Construction of
present structure:**
1895

Location:
In 7 feet of water, off Solomons
Lump (about 150 feet south of
the remains of the earlier
screwpile lighthouse), on the
south side of Kedges Strait,
Maryland, between the
Chesapeake Bay and Tangier
Sound.

Position:
38 02 (50)
76 00 (52)

Characteristic of light:
Flashing white, 6-second
interval; 2 red sectors from 086
to 111 degrees and from 288 to
294 degrees; obscured from
331.5 to 039 degrees.

**Height of light, above
mean high water:**
47 feet.

Range:
White, 8 miles; red, 6 miles.

Description of station:
Brown cylindrical foundation
pier surmounted by a white
brick tower (and formerly, a
two-story lighthouse dwelling
which, together with the square
lighthouse tower formed a
regular octagonal building).

The following year, construction on the new lighthouse was begun and, somewhat belatedly ("after mature consideration," the Board reported), it was decided that a caisson structure would be highly preferable to another lighthouse of screwpile design. The only obstacle was money. The Board suggested that money saved by an "advantageous contract" for the construction of Wolf Trap lighthouse could be used to make up the difference in cost, "if Congress would authorize the use of this balance for the purpose..." Their request was granted in December 1893.

As construction on the new lighthouse began, the wreck of the screwpile was carried away by ice and the temporary light had to be discontinued. "[T]here is nothing left from which a light can be exhibited..." an alarmed Board reported in April of 1895.

The caisson, assembled at the Lazaretto lighthouse depot, was loaded onto a barge in May of 1895 and towed to Solomons Lump. "The caisson was anchored in position at 9 a.m. on May 20, and the work of sinking was begun," the Board reported.

> On May 31 it had reached its proper depth, but was somewhat out of level. Attempts were made to bring the structure to an even bearing, and with success, but not until it had sunk about 2 feet 6 inches below the specified depth. An additional section of cylinder was procured in order to give the structure its proper height above water level. Concrete was filled in to about 6 feet above high-water line, the cellar and cisterns were constructed, and on June 30, 1895, the foundation cylinder was completed and the erection of the superstructure was begun.

In September of 1895, the house was completed and its fixed white light, in a fifth-order Fresnel lens, was exhibited for the first time.

The octagonal lantern with a circular metal roof and ventilator ball sat atop a square tower with wrought-iron balustrades. The tower formed two sides of the octagonal structure, each side of which was nine feet long (thus, the tower sits to one side of the caisson, a fact which is all the more noticeable now that the two-story dwelling has been removed). Rather than constructing the iron plates to flare outward towards the top of the caisson (like the trumpet-shaped caissons of Baltimore Light and Point No Point), it appears that the covered gallery deck of Solomons Lump was actually cantilevered beyond the rim. The first level of the dwelling contained the kitchen, living room and work space; the second level accommodated two bedrooms.

Located just south of Bloodsworth Island, in an area that was the hangout of pirates in colonial times (and today is the refuge of much Chesapeake Bay wildlife), Solomons Lump is perhaps the loneliest lighthouse on the Chesapeake Bay. As the seafood industry has declined, the number of boats going in and out of Crisfield has likewise dwindled and the lighthouse is probably seen by fewer mariners each year. Until radio and telephone communications were installed on the light (beginning in the 1920's), there was no direct connection between the keeper and assistant keeper of Solomons Lump and the shore. Thus, during fog and winter storms, the keepers' families worried continuously that the lighthouse might be rammed by a ship, damaged by ice, or, even, that the keeper might fall victim to foul play (as happened to the keeper of the Holland Bar Light who was mysteriously murdered in 1931). Likewise, there was always concern for the keeper on his eight-mile one-way trip to shore, a trip that was made in a small skiff, and—given that the keeper and assistant keeper always looked forward to their shore leave—was generally made with little regard for the weather.

For many years—in fact, for most of the period from 1900 until 1937—Solomons Lump was under the care of Henry Columbus Sterling. His trips to and from the lighthouse were a source of worry to his family. Sterling made the eight-mile trip in a tiny sailboat.

"During the great freeze of 1936," the *Crisfield's Times* reported in a retrospective on Sterling's life,

> *when the Jane's Island light was swept away, there was great concern for the safety of Sterling and his Solomon's Lump Light. Finally his son, in a desperate attempt to ascertain if the lighthouse was still intact, climbed to the top of the Crisfield Ice Plant, saw the light still burning and knew that his father was safe. Actually, Sterling had abandoned the lighthouse and walked across the ice to Smith Island. In doing this, Sterling refused to leave the lighthouse until he was ordered in writing to do so by his next higher eschelon of command. This was dropped to him by plane shortly thereafter.*

In April of 1950, Solomons Lump light was changed to unwatched operation and shortly thereafter the dwelling was demolished. The condition of the light station began to deteriorate rapidly. In 1988 the exterior of the lighthouse tower was given superficial maintenance by the crew of the U.S. Coast Guard Cutter Chokecherry: a combined sealer and paint coating was applied to the masonry and the upper part of the caisson foundation was scraped and painted by hand (though sandblasting of the entire caisson foundation above the water line had been the recommendation). Yellowed acrylic panels were removed from the lantern and plate glass was reinstalled giving greater clarity to the light. Additionally, cracks were filled on the caisson deck and the surface was coated with roofing material with the hope that this would deter leaks into the interior of the foundation.

Point Lookout

The Point Lookout lighthouse is a bay light that from 1830 to 1965 marked the north entrance to the Potomac River. As early as 1825, $1,800 was appropriated by Congress for a small beacon light on Point Lookout. Described by a naval officer from the district of Baltimore as "but a bleak, barren sand beach for many acres," the owner of the acreage which the lighthouse service proposed to buy protested the amount that was offered ($500), and a group of freeholders was selected to set a value (by warrant from the St. Mary's commissioners to the county sheriff). When all was said and done, Jenifer Taylor was apparently paid $1100 for the lighthouse property, but the deal was not finalized until 1833, three years after the lighthouse was first commissioned (and Taylor then claimed that interest was owed on the original price). In the meantime, the Fifth Auditor, Samuel Pleasanton—a man whose obstinate determination to see the lighthouse built was apparently a good match for Taylor's stubborn refusal to accept payment—simply decided to go ahead with erection of the station.

In 1828, $4,500 was appropriated for the small lighthouse. Built by John Donahoo, the original structure was a diminutive white house with a red shingle roof and black lantern on top of the dwelling. The idea of using gas rather than oil to light the lamp was experimented with but soon abandoned. In July 1830, the new lighthouse was inspected and met with approval except for the fact that cast iron rather than wrought iron had been used for the lantern. The light was commissioned on September 30, 1830.

In 1883 the original lighthouse dwelling with its rooftop lantern (commissioned in 1853) was enlarged and the light station, midway between the Portsmouth and Lazaretto depots, was also selected to become a buoy depot. Photo, U.S. Coast Guard.

The first keeper, James Davis, died only two months after assuming his post and was succeeded by his wife, Ann Davis, who kept the light until 1848. Records show that a scant six months after her appointment she was told that she could not be allowed to sell liquor on the premises—apparently an entrepreneurial oversight on her part which happily left no permanent blemish on her service record for she went on to become a well-regarded keeper. The next keeper, William Wood, did not fare quite so well in the eyes of the lighthouse service: a cat fell into the oil barrel, spoiling 56 gallons of lamp oil, and he broke 24 glass lamp chimneys that were packed in a crate in the basement. Wood's 1849 pay was withheld.

Over the years, several women keepers were associated with the light: Martha Edwards (1853-1855) and Pamela Edwards (1855-1869) who weathered the Civil War when a federal prisoner-of-war camp and hospital for Union soldiers were constructed on the point. In 1863, Civil War nurse Sarah Blunt

Michael Ventura

Light station established:
1830

**Construction of
present structure:**
Enlarged in 1880's and lantern
raised.

Location:
On Point Lookout, Maryland,
north side of the entrance to
the Potomac River, west side of
the Chesapeake Bay.

Position:
38 02 19
76 19 20

Characteristic of light:
Inactive.

**Height of light, above
mean high water:**
41 feet.

Description of station:
White dwelling, trimmed in
red.

wrote to a friend from Point Lookout where she was stationed at Hammond Hospital...

> *I don't think you can come down to the Point. It being a military station. There are no boarding houses. You might though in case of an emergency come and stay at the lighthouse. .... [O]ur walks have been down to the point where the lighthouse stands. The other roads are in too dreadful a condition for us to attempt it without India rubber boots which I am the only fortunate possessor of.*

There were many complaints about the callous treatment of the Confederate soldiers, nearly 4,000 of whom died over a 16-month period and were buried near the lighthouse. The ambivalence and pain of these years and the tragic loss of human life appear to live on in ghostly memory, for apparently almost everyone who has spent any time at the lighthouse since it was decommissioned by the Coast Guard is ready to testify that it is haunted. It is the only Chesapeake Bay lighthouse that has been investigated by a full-fledged team of paranormal psychologists.

The focal plane of the original Point Lookout light was only 24 feet. The structure was later raised by the addition of a second story, giving the lantern, which rests just below the peak of the hipped roof on the front side of the house, a height of 41 feet above mean high tide. In the 1850's a fourth-order Fresnel lens was installed with an arc of 300 degrees. The light had a visibility of almost 12 miles.

In 1855, the Light-House Board reported that the keeper's dwelling had been thoroughly repaired and remarked that a new fence would be required as "the posts and rails of the old fence are almost all decayed." In 1858 an inspector reported that the brick masonry was painted yellow and the tower white—the red shingled roof remained unchanged. In later years, the house was once again painted white and the lantern black. In 1860 a Franklin lamp was substituted for the old valve lamp and, in 1872, the Board reported that they had "commenced the work of establishing a large fog bell" at Point Lookout. "This is a very desirable aid to navigation," the Board noted, "and will be equally valuable to vessels navigating the bay and river." The fog bell tower was built and outfitted with a 1000-pound bell cast at Mencely Foundry, West Troy, New York (the bell is now housed at the Chesapeake Bay Maritime Museum, St. Michaels, Maryland). The bell, struck by machinery at 10 second intervals, was finished and in operation by November of 1872.

In 1883 the roof was removed, the additional story was added, and new porches were built on the front and back of the dwelling—outfitting the lighthouse dwelling for two keepers and their families. At this time, the entire building was stuccoed. "The station," the Board wrote, "is now in excellent order."

Because of the distance between the Lazaretto and Portsmouth depots, Point Lookout was also made a buoy depot in 1883, and the construction of coal and buoy sheds necessitated moving the fog bell tower a few years later because there were complaints that it could no longer be heard—"[o]wing to the fact," the Board wrote in 1888, "that the coal and buoy sheds are higher than the fog-bell tower [and] intercept the sound." That same year, the Board complained that "water had encroached so far upon the river front of the lighthouse tract as to cover one end of the foundation of one of the buildings of the depot." Emergency measures were taken and a temporary breakwater was constructed by depositing several hundred barrels of "damaged cement" from Fort Washington along the bank, but the Board requested an appropriation of $500 for construction of a more "permanent breakwater of timber or stone."

The following year construction of the breakwater was begun, a new stable and summer-kitchen were added, and a new fog bell striking apparatus was purchased and installed. In 1894 an iron oil house, "capable of storing about 1,000 gallons of mineral oil," was procured and it was erected at the site the following year. In 1899, "new-model fourth-order lamps" were supplied.

In 1910, the year that the Light-House Board was disbanded and the service was transferred to the newly established Bureau of Lighthouses in the Department of Commerce, reports indicate that the wharf was in bad condition and that no repairs were made. Apparently civilian keepers continued to man Point Lookout after it was transferred to the U.S. Coast Guard in 1939. The keepers included Westley Fulcher, Herman Metivier, Marvin Fulcher, Wallace Sturgis and George Gatton.

The U.S. Navy began purchasing land around the lighthouse in 1951 and when, in 1965, the U.S. Coast Guard replaced the lantern light with an off-shore steel tower, it was only a matter of two months before the Point Lookout light station was turned over to the U.S. Navy. For a number of years, the State of Maryland maintained a lease on the property and the dwelling was occupied and cared for, but the lease was relinquished in 1980 because of problems with the water system which the U.S. Navy declined to correct. For the past fifteen years, the Navy has shown no apparent interest in maintaining the historic structure—and has refused to allow it to be rented on the grounds that the property is unfit for habitation. Apparently, what little maintenance there is—a general once-a-year sprucing up in preparation for an annual open house hosted by Point Lookout State Park—has been undertaken by the Maryland park service with volunteer help. (In fact, inquiries regarding the lighthouse to the public affairs office of the Patuxent Naval Air Station are referred to Point Lookout State Park.) In recent years, the State of Maryland has made repeated efforts to acquire the Point Lookout lighthouse for restoration and to make it part of Point Lookout State Park. The future of this historic lighthouse—which now sits on a fenced installation with a radio tower nearby that is used as a tracking station and is considered to be part of the naval air station's defense system—is uncertain. One thing is incontrovertible: the lighthouse structure, one of the oldest on the Chesapeake Bay, is presently on a downslide.

Piney Point

In March of 1835, Congress appropriated $5,000 for construction of a lighthouse at Piney Point (so-named for the loblolly and long-leaf yellow pines which abounded along the shoreline) on the Maryland side of the Potomac River, 14 miles upstream from the mouth of the Potomac on the Chesapeake Bay. The lighthouse, the oldest of 11 lighthouses which once aided mariners along the Potomac River, was intended to replace a lightship which had been in operation at the site since 1821 to warn mariners of dangerous shoals at Piney Point and across the Potomac at Ragged Point. Today, only three of eleven lighthouses built on the Potomac River remain: Piney Point, Jones Point and Fort Washington. Piney Point was the first to be built.

Between 1820 and 1910, Piney Point was the summertime social center of Washington, D.C. President James Monroe maintained a summer cottage at Piney Point (known as "The Summer White House") and there were many other notable vacationers: Daniel Webster, John C. Calhoun and Henry Clay were all guests of the Piney Point Hotel (forced to close following a 1933 hurricane) who enjoyed the summertime bathing and fishing which this Potomac River spot offered; Presidents Franklin Pierce and Teddy Roosevelt also escaped the heat of Washington D.C. at Piney Point. During World War II, Piney Point became the testing range for torpedoes manufactured in Alexandria, Virginia. Following the war, the Naval Torpedo Test Center and Range was decommissioned and the base became known as the Pane Hall Center of the Harry Lundeberg School of Seamanship.

On Christmas Eve of 1835, a deed to 2.57 acres at Piney Point was obtained from Henry Suter and his wife at a cost of $300. In September of 1836 John Donahoo completed the construction and the light was commissioned. For over 125 years thereafter the light guided vessels along the Potomac River.

Similar in design to Donahoo's other lighthouses, the Piney Point lighthouse is a squat masonry tower in the form of a truncated cone, 30 feet from its base

The fog bell tower, constructed in 1880, was destroyed by Hurricane Hazel in 1954 and has never been rebuilt. In this photo the diaphone which replaced the fog bell (still visible on the roof) as the low-visibility signal of choice points towards the Potomac River. Photo (c. 1937), U.S. Coast Guard.

to the center of the lantern (according to 19th-century light lists), with a height above mean high tide of approximately 34 feet. The tower is painted white and the lantern, traditionally black, has been painted an attractive brick red in the years since it was deactivated by the U.S. Coast Guard as a navigational aid.

In 1855, the old reflecting apparatus—ten lamps and ten 15-inch reflectors with a visibility of 10 miles—was replaced with a more efficient 5th-order Fresnel lens, increasing the light's visibility a full mile. Twenty-five years later, in 1880, a thirty-foot bell tower, painted white, was added to the light station to protect mariners from fog which often accumulated along the shoreline. The fog bell, located 15 feet to the west of the tower, had an automatic

Michael Ventura (Photo shortly before restoration.)

81

Light station established:
1836

**Construction of
present structure:**
1836

Location:
On Piney Point, Maryland,
northeast side of the Potomac
River, about 12 miles northwest of Point Lookout.

Position:
38 08 07
76 31 48

Characteristic of light:
Inactive. St. Clement's Island-
Potomac River Museum
illuminates the lantern.

**Height of light, above
mean high water:**
34 feet.

Description of station:
White tower and detached
dwelling; red lantern.

striking device. In 1936 the fog bell was replaced by a reed horn. The bell tower was destroyed by Hurricane Hazel in 1954 and was never rebuilt.

Perhaps the squattest of the sturdy and stocky Donahoo lighthouse towers (all of which exhibit more rugged resolve than architectural grace), the Piney Point light station has a story book, gnome-like appearance. The enduring towers built by John Donahoo and his assistant, Winslow Lewis, are also testimony to the penny-pinching pragmatism of the Fifth Auditor of the Treasury, Stephen Pleasanton, who guided the U.S. lighthouse establishment for thirty years. Both Donahoo and Lewis consistently bid low and built to a standard construction design (no architects were consulted)—and thus conformed to the preferred *modus operandi* of Pleasanton. In this sense, the Piney Point light epitomizes the values of Fifth Auditor—a serviceable light with no monumental pretensions.

According to the Maryland Historical Trust's report, the interior diameter of the tower is 13 feet at ground level with walls approximately 48 inches wide. These dimensions reduce to an interior diameter of approximately seven feet just below the lantern deck with walls that are 18 inches wide. The tower has a small five-foot entrance door with stone door jambs and a single-stone threshold, and there are three windows at different elevations as one ascends the tower. The lighthouse floor is constructed of brick pavers. A spiral wooden stairway, constructed around a central column with the exterior (or outboard) of the wooden treads embedded in the brick masonry, leads to the top of the tower where a masonry vault supports the lantern deck. The wooden stair treads, lintels and window sills are generally in poor condition; many of them are rotted or missing. One enters the nine-sided lantern by climbing an iron ship's ladder through an opening in the lantern deck which has an iron trap door. The lantern panes are rectangular and the iron framing of the lantern is covered by a standing seam metal roof and capped with a large ventilator ball. The Fresnel lens has been removed though the tower is sometimes illuminated at night and the original light pedestal remains in the lantern. The floor of the lantern is constructed of stone wedges, radially laid; the parapet wall is masonry, approximately 54 inches high, with an iron half door that provides access to an exterior brick masonry ledge, approximately 14 inches wide. The lantern deck is cantilevered a few inches beyond the rim of the tower and an iron railing, approximately 40 inches high, is set in concrete that slopes away from the brick ledge to the cantilevered stone of the underlying lantern deck. Some spalling has occurred on the gallery ledge and the concrete is in poor condition. On the whole, the masonry of the tower is in fair condition, however, and the mortar joints are sound.

As built by Donahoo in 1836, the original keeper's dwelling was one story with an A-line roof, measuring approximately 30 by 20 feet. The tiny house included a central fireplace, parlor, dining room and cellar. A small 10-by-12-foot kitchen was added sometime later. In 1884, the three-room dwelling was enlarged by the addition of a second story. In 1930, the Light-House Service estimated the value of the buildings and land as follows: lighthouse, $5,600.00; fog-signal house, $780.00; oilhouse, $500.00; storehouse, $450.00; dwelling, $4,200.00; appraised value of land $1,000.00; and improvements, $11,530.00.

When the Piney Point light was decommissioned in 1964, the Coast Guard continued to use the station for personnel housing for a number of years. In 1980, the U.S. Coast Guard transferred ownership of the lighthouse property to St. Mary's County and the Department of Recreation and Parks took over the site and placed it under the jurisdiction of the St. Clement's Island-Potomac River Museum, 20 miles away at Cotton Point. (The museum was recently honored with accreditation by the American Association of Museums.) The St. Clement's Island-Potomac River Museum has begun an ambitious program of beautification and restoration of the lighthouse property and tower. Recently, the Steuart Petroleum Company, which adjoins the lighthouse station, donated $11,000 to the Foundation of the Friends of the St. Clement's Island-Potomac River Museum and these funds were used—among other things—on external lighting, repointing of bricks on the keeper's quarters, upgrading of restrooms to meet the standards of the American Disabilities Act, and the installation of benches and picnic tables and landscaping. Additionally, the museum has just completed a charming boardwalk that leads directly from the keeper's quarters to the pier on the Potomac River where a narrow, sandy beach and broad belt of pine and wild growth offer an appealing contrast to the more manicured landscaping that surrounds the lighthouse proper. Smaller boardwalks flank flower beds around the lighthouse lawn and are illuminated with lanterns on posts festooned with hanging baskets of flowers during the summer months. Well-placed exhibit panels tell the history of the light station. Although the keeper's dwelling is privately rented, the park is now open to the public from sunrise to sundown and offers a delightful picnic area, a beautiful view of the Potomac River, and a small museum gift shop staffed by volunteers. The future of this historic lighthouse complex is bright.

Fort Washington

The diminutive wooden light and fog bell tower of the light station at Fort Washington on the Potomac River is primarily of interest because of the history of the fort on which it stands. The fort, first proposed by George Washington after the establishment of the federal city on the Potomac River, was originally called Fort Warburton, after Warburton Manor (the estate of William Digges, situated directly across the Potomac from Mount Vernon). William Digges and his son, George Digges, were friends of General Washington's and apparently often sent one of their boats to pick him up for dinner. Washington would stand on a small embankment in front of his home and wave a flag whereupon Digges would dispatch a boat rowed by his slaves from his dock on the other side of the river. In his 1862 book, *Life of George Washington*, Washington Irving says that such scenes of "ostentation among the rich planters" living along the banks of the Potomac were not infrequent, and specifically mentions "Mr. Digges who always received Washington in his barge, rowed by 6 negroes, arrayed in a kind of uniform of check shirts and black velvet caps."

In 1798, when war threatened with France, a preliminary survey of Warburton Point (or Digges Point) was made with a view to construction of a fort on the site, but construction waited another 10 years when, once again, tensions with the belligerent nations of Britain and France prompted serious attention to the defense of American seacoast and waterways. This time four acres were purchased and the fortification was finally built. The original fortification presented an elliptical front to the river with semicircular flanks. The back of the garrison was enclosed with a wall. Apparently, however, the fort was neither well-positioned in relation to the main channel of the river, nor was it well-defended from ground attack.

During the War of 1812, the British first attempted to send warships up the Potomac in 1813, but they were grounded at Kettle Bottom Shoals, leading the Americans to the erroneous view that the large vessels of the British fleet could not navigate the Potomac to Washington, D.C. By then, much of the main channel had been heavily silted by construction projects along the riverbanks—including the construction of the fort—and the once-lively fishing industry had begun a precipitous decline ("...ruined," one observer reported, "by the envelopment of dry earth and other obstructions consequent to the Fort"). Thus, when in August of 1814 British vessels began to bombard the fort from their anchorage just off Mount Vernon, they found no resistance. Instead, they were astounded by a tremendous explosion and discovered the next day that the fort had been abandoned and the ammunition and explosives storehouse detonated. Not surprisingly, the officer in charge of Fort Warburton, Captain Samuel T. Dyson, was court martialed and discharged. The fort was rebuilt (architect and engi-

The Fort Washington light is actually displayed in the fog bell tower. The distinctive keeper's house and outbuildings have unfortunately been torn down. Photo (c. 1940), U.S. Coast Guard.

Starke Jett

85

Today the lighthouse is off-limits to the public, but in the 1950's it was a popular recreational spot where on warm summer days visitors could even buy a soda and hot dog. Photo, U.S. Coast Guard.

neer Pierre L'Enfant supervised the beginning of its reconstruction), and by 1824 it was completed essentially as it remains today, administered as a public monument by the National Park Service.

During this early period, there was no lighthouse at the point (formed by the intersection of the Potomac with Swan and Piscataway Creeks) to guide vessels along the river channel. It was not until November 7, 1856, that then-Secretary of War Jefferson Davis (soon to become president of the Confederacy) communicated with the Secretary of the Treasury regarding the Light-House Board's request that a small beacon be placed near the landing at Fort Washington. "...I have the honor to inform you," Davis wrote, "that your request is granted on condition that the light shall be placed upon the wharf and not within any of the fortifications; and that the light keeper shall be subordinate to the military command of the post and public ground in all that relates to police and discipline."

Because only $500 had been appropriated by Congress, the light built was a temporary one (hardly qualifying as a lighthouse)—an eighteen-and-one-half foot cast-iron column with a light so small that protests were soon forthcoming. In 1869, the Light-House Board reported that "[c]omplaint having been made of the inadequacy of this light, it is proposed to improve it." The following year, the Board noted that "the framework of a beacon-light to replace the temporary post and lantern at Fort Washington" had been completed at the Lazaretto workshops in December. "In February," the Board continued, "the steam-tender Tulip, with a party and the necessary supplies and appliances, proceeded to the locality for the purpose of putting up the beacon. This structure, furnished with a lens of the sixth order and a lantern of the portable beacon pattern, was completed on the 18th [of] February."

86

In 1882, a 32-foot fog-bell tower was erected at the station, and when, in 1883, permission was received from Secretary of War Robert Lincoln "to erect on the land belonging to Fort Washington, Maryland, a small wooden structure suitable for a keeper's dwelling," the plans and specifications were finally drawn up. "The construction is delayed," the Board noted, "by more important works in hand, but it will soon be undertaken. All the material was delivered and is now stored at the Lazaretto depot or at the site."

The house was finished in January of 1885, and, besides repairs and improvements to the keeper's living quarters (a brick cistern for drinking water and 30 running feet of whitewashed picket fence), there is little mention of the lighthouse until 1900 when the Light-House Board complained that "[t]he tower should be built about 6 or 8 feet higher than the present one, that the light may show above a structure which has recently been erected at the military post here by the War Department." In addition, the Board noted that "[t]he lantern of the tower is small and its ventilation is poor." The Board asked for an appropriation of $1600 to construct a new tower. No appropriation was forthcoming, however, and in late 1901 the engineers of the Fifth District took matters into their own hands. "To increase the range of visibility of this light by placing it at a greater elevation, and as a temporary expedient," the Board noted in its annual report, "four new caps were put on the sills of the fog-bell tower...and a platform was built on them to support a lens lantern." The new light, about 28 feet above mean high water (twice as high as the earlier light), was exhibited from the fog bell tower in January. Nevertheless, the Board continued to request funds for the erection of a new tower. Meanwhile, the old iron tower was torn down.

The fort, essentially obsolete after the Civil War, was abandoned in 1872 but reactivated in 1896 when, with the threat of war with England, the 4th Artillery Battery "M" arrived with 90 men to place three Rodman smooth-bore guns in position at the fort. The battery commanded an electrically controlled mine field and used electricity for communication with other batteries (which thus could be more widely dispersed and better concealed). Then, in 1921, the 12th Infantry was moved to Fort Washington, but since by now the fort had little military value, it was transferred to the Department of the Interior in 1939 and soon placed under the administration of the National Park Service. Although Fort Washington is open to the public, the lighthouse and bell-tower, painted white with fluorescent warning signs, is off-limits and now surrounded by a fence. The light was automated early in the 20th century and the Bureau of Lighthouses removed its keeper. Unfortunately, the very attractive keeper's complex has been torn down.

Light station established: 1857
Construction of present structure: 1882
Location: On the wharf at Fort Washington, Maryland, east side of the Potomac River.
Position: 38 42 44 77 02 14
Characteristic of light: Flashing red, 6-second interval.
Height of light, above mean high water: 28 feet.
Range: 7 miles.
Description of station: Lantern on white and orange wooden tower.

Jones Point

In 1852, the Light-House Board secured an appropriation of $5,000 to purchase land and construct a lighthouse at Jones Point. The light station was intended to warn ships entering the ports of Alexandria, Georgetown, and Washington City away from sandbars in the river. In April of 1855, a plot of land at the tip of Jones Point, 30 feet by 100 feet (and including one of the original boundary stones of the "Territory of Columbia" laid on April 15, 1791), was sold for $501 to the federal government by The Manassas Gap Rail Road Company for the purpose of establishing a light station.

In the mid-19th century, the bustling port of Alexandria, Virginia was the third largest harbor on the Chesapeake Bay's navigational system and was especially in need of a beacon to guide incoming vessels. In fact, by that time, the area had been a center for commerce and trade for over two hundred years. Published accounts of the natural wealth of the area—beginning with those of Captain John Smith who sailed up the Potomac in June of 1608—had attracted many settlers in the 17th century when trade with the Indians in beaver pelts was brisk. Cadwalder Jones, an English trader and mapmaker, built a cabin at Jones Point in 1699, a time when tobacco trade was just beginning to supplant the fur trade. By the end of the 18th century, wheat had overtaken tobacco as the major export commodity and this change—along with the establishment of many mills and bakeries—brought increased prosperity to the new town of Alexandria.

The Jones Point light station, probably in the late 19th century. In this photo the configuration of the point is still visible. Photo, The National Archives.

The lighthouse, constructed by Charles B. Church, was wooden clapboard, painted white. A pitched cedar roof supported the black lantern (a circular turret with a wrought-iron catwalk) whose first illumination was visible for nine miles.

"BRILLIANT," *The Alexandria Gazette* reported on May 4, 1856, the morning after the lamp was first lit. From the beginning, the lighthouse was a local attraction and gathering place for Alexandria residents. In the summertime good fishing and the pleasant pastoral setting brought recreational parties of fishermen, swimmers, boaters and picnickers. In the wintertime, frozen ice and the dazzling illumination of the lighthouse made it an ideal spot for ice-skating. According to some, the buoy shed near the lighthouse was also a popular recreational retreat—for gambling and for imbibing Maryland rye or Virginia corn whiskey. Some say that a poker game, under the aegis of keeper Benjamin Potter Greenwood, went on in the basement of the lighthouse during the entire four years of the Civil War.

According to the records of the Mount Vernon chapter of the Daughters of the American Revolution, George L. Deston and J.P. Geisendoffer were lightkeepers between 1856 and 1866 when, at the age of 21, Benjamin Porter Greenwood moved in as lightkeeper and remained (marrying twice and ap-

Starke Jett

parently fathering 14 children) until his death in 1903. Thus, his life is coterminous with the most active days of the light station. His second wife and her family remained until 1906 when the station was taken over by Frank Wilkins. Wilkins remained until shortly after World War I.

During the first years of the lighthouse, whale oil lamps were used for the light, but in 1858, the city of Alexandria pressured the Light-House Board to permit gas lines to be laid from the Alexandria Gas Works. Thus it came to pass that a gas light burned in the lantern—though erosion and water caused almost constant difficulties with the pipe line—until 1900, when mineral oil lamps were once again placed in the 5th-order Fresnel lens. Also in 1900, the fixed white light was changed to fixed red by the insertion of ruby lamp chimneys—a change which caused some consternation and confusion since the light-house was now in the vicinity of Alexandria's red-light district. Once again, in 1919, the characteristic of the light was changed to flashing white and its brilliance was quadrupled when a 200-candlepower flashing acetylene light was placed about one hundred yards from the lighthouse on the farthest point of land reaching into the river. Even so, a landfill operation at Battery Cove had greatly limited the usefulness of the light to vessels on the Potomac.

During WWII, the caretakers of Jones Point, the Mount Vernon Chapter of the Daughters of the American Revolution, were denied access to the light by the U.S. Army Signal Corps. When they regained possession after the war, they found the light in pitiable condition. Photo (c. 1950), U.S. Coast Guard.

In 1926, a skeletal steel tower with a fixed green light was erected on the new shoreline. That same year, the Jones Point lighthouse was turned over to the Mount Vernon Chapter of the Daughters of the American Revolution who, according to their accounts, completed a thorough restoration of the dwelling and installed a custodian. The last resident was a Mrs. McMahan, who used the lighthouse as a studio for her "Sport Doll Factory." McMahan kept the lighthouse open to the public until 1936 when the U.S. Army Signal Corps surrounded the lighthouse and its grounds with wire fencing, effectively forcing her to leave. Because of the secret nature of the Signal Corps' radio station, the D.A.R. was denied access to the lighthouse during the Second World War. At the end of the war, it was returned to the custody of the D.A.R. in wretched condition. The walls of the modest lighthouse had been used for target practice and the interior was gutted. The tower was automated in 1934 and discontinued in November of 1962. Now the lights of the Woodrow Wilson Bridge serve to orient boaters.

Over the past few years, a tremendous amount of hope and hard work has gone into restoration of the lighthouse dwelling, the combined effort of volunteers, the National Park Service and the Mount Vernon chapter of Daughters of the American Revolution. Funds for the project have been scant and the results have been mixed. The lighthouse property is easily accessible and vandalism will almost certainly remain a serious problem unless a caretaker takes up residence at the lighthouse. Close to the abutment of the Woodrow Wilson Bridge (which apparently often serves as a temporary shelter for vagrants), the lighthouse property has also been occupied by the homeless, and on more than one occasion the interior of the dwelling has been damaged by fire.

The Mount Vernon chapter of the D.A.R. has worked hard to secure the future of the Jones Point lighthouse. In the mid-1960's 3,000 square feet of property, including the lighthouse and the boundary stone, was deeded to the Department of the Interior. The agreement stipulated that the lighthouse would be restored and that the surrounding area would be turned into a park. Today a 50-acre park with walking and biking trails—owned by the National Park Service and maintained by the city of Alexandria—does surround the lighthouse, but restoration of the property was not acccomplished under the terms of the agreement and, once again, in the 1980's the Mount Vernon Chapter entered into negotiations with the Department of Interior. As has been the case with many Chesapeake Bay lighthouses, red tape and competing interests have hampered efforts at restoration. In the 1980's local officials successfully warded off an attempt by the federal government to sell the land to real estate developers and, finally, in 1986, a joint agreement was signed with the National Park Service to restore the lighthouse as an interpretive museum.

Although the Mount Vernon chapter of the D.A.R. has relinquished ownership of the lighthouse, they have not ceased in their effort to raise money for its restoration. The first requirement of restoration was actually the construction of a new sea wall—an expensive undertaking that was accomplished with money raised locally and with a matching state grant. As of this writing, the exterior of the building has been restored and the light once again shines from the rooftop latern and will henceforth appear on navigational maps. Restoration of the interior, however, is not yet complete and trespassing continues to be a problem—on a pleasant afternoon it is not unusual to find picnickers with their hibachis set up on the front porch, enjoying the fresh air and the view of the river.

Light station established:
1855

Construction of present structure:
1855

Location:
On Jones Point, Virginia (no longer configured as a point because of land fill along the river), west bank of the Potomac River, about one mile below Alexandria.

Position:
38 47 25
77 02 27

Characteristic of light:
Inactive. D.A.R. and National Park Service illuminate.

Height of light, above mean high water:
28 feet.

Description of station:
Black lantern on white frame dwelling.

Smith Point

A total of five lighthouses have been erected at Smith Point near the mouth of the Potomac River on the Virginia side, and numerous light vessels have been stationed in the waters nearby. The first lighthouse was built in 1802, but no more than five years later it had to be moved inland. Even so, the mainland light proved ineffective, and, in 1821, a lightship was placed in service within a few miles of the lighthouse.

Once again, in 1828, shore erosion necessitated the purchase of additional land and the construction of a new tower further inland. The new lighthouse was poorly constructed and by 1853 was in extremely dilapidated condition—the tower, now only 35 feet from the bank, was badly cracked and the lantern's iron frame was dangerously weakened. "The cost to put this establishment in order would be great," the Light-House Board noted in its annual report. "With a view to economy and utility," the Board recommended construction of a screwpile lighthouse "near the end of the spit making off from that point," but when Congress made an appropriation in 1854, the sum was deemed "wholly inadequate to the erection of a suitable and durable structure at that exposed place." In 1855, 5th-District lighthouse inspector A.M. Pennock reported that a new fourth-order Fresnel lens had been installed to replace the "old reflecting apparatus consisting of 15 lamps and 15 sixteen-inch reflectors." "Before putting up a fourth order Fresnel lens at this station," he wrote, "I had the tower, lantern, and keeper's dwelling—which were in a wretched condition—put into temporary repair, sufficient to preserve the new apparatus," but, he noted somewhat pessimistically, "the bank on which the tower stands is fast washing away..."

In 1857, the Light-House Board reported that the light vessel at Smith Point had been replaced with "a better vessel, fitted with the best illuminating apparatus that can be used." "The light-vessel," the Board continued, "not only marks the extremity of the Smith's Point shoal, but serves also as a guide to the entrance of the Potomac River, independently of the light-house on Point Lookout." Thus, the Board noted that the mainland lighthouse was no longer of any utility—"the foundation upon which it is built is wearing away by the constant abrasion of the tides, rendering frequent expenditures upon it and the tower necessary"—and they recommended that it be discontinued.

In 1859, the mainland light was removed and a family was allowed to rent the premises in return for maintaining the grounds. The lightship remained in service for another two years when it was destroyed by Confederate guerrillas. Promptly in 1862, however, a newly outfitted ship was placed in service until, in 1868, the screwpile lighthouse was finally completed (according to the regulations of the Light-House Board requiring the substitution of lighthouses for light vessels).

The screwpile structure fared well for 25 years. In 1869, the character of the light was changed from fixed white to revolving white. That same year, a glass pane, broken by waterfowl, had to be replaced. In 1882, the fog signal

In the 1960's, Smith Point still kept its backup fog bell, but the lantern deck now also sports radio and television antennas, adding an odd touch to the lighthouse silhouette. Photo, U.S. Coast Guard.

Starke Jett

Light station established:
1868

**Construction of
present structure:**
1897

Location:
In 20 feet of water, on the
west side of Chesapeake Bay,
Virginia, about two-and-one-
half miles east-southeast of
Smith Point, on the south
side of the mouth of the
Potomac River.

Position:
37 52 47
76 11 02

Characteristic of light:
Flashing white, 10-second
interval; red sector from 003
to 156 degrees.

**Height of light, above
mean high water:**
52 feet.

Range:
White, 22 miles; red, 18
miles.

Description of station:
Brown cylindrical foundation
pier expanding in trumpet
shape at its upper end to form
a gallery; white octagonal
two-story brick dwelling with
square tower rising from the
roof on the south side; black
lantern.

Fog signal:
Horn: 1 blast every 15
seconds (2-second blast),
operating continuously.

was moved to the roof and placed in a specially constructed room to improve its audibility. The station was outfitted with boat-hoisters and was, the Board reported, "thoroughly repaired." In 1893, the station was badly damaged by ice. "The keepers," the Board reported, "abandoned the station when the danger seemed imminent, and the light was temporarily discontinued." (The damage was repaired, but the keepers were dismissed.) Then, on February 14, 1895, the lighthouse was ripped from the foundation and carried away. "The illuminating and fog-bell apparatus, some oil, and a few small articles of supply were recovered from the wreck," the Board continued, "and stored at the Lazaretto light-house depot." An appropriation of $25,000 was quickly made by Congress to begin work on the construction of a new lighthouse. Congress also authorized the Board to make contracts up to the amount of $80,000 for reestablishment of the light station.

A caisson lighthouse was decided upon and borings were made at the proposed site. The metal work was promptly completed and delivered to the Lazaretto depot. In September 1896, construction of the wooden caisson began at a Baltimore City dock. "On November 17, 1896," the Board reported, "it was successfully launched, and during March it was completed to towing trim with two sections of the cast-iron cylinder and the air shaft carried up to a height of 18 feet from the roof of the air chamber." In April, the Board continued, "a start was made for the site, which was reached ten days later, after some time had been spent in harbor at the mouth of the Great Wicomico River awaiting favorable conditions." While they waited, the construction workers deposited another three feet of concrete to the 13 inches already filling the cylinder. The structure was grounded in position on April 17, surrounded with 150 tons of riprap stone, and within a few hours had settled of its own accord about two feet into the shoal.

By the end of April, the fifth course of cylinder plates had been finished and concrete deposited to within six inches of the top. The pneumatic machinery was then readied to sink the caisson which on May 22 reached the required depth of 15 feet 5 inches. "In penetrating the last 3 feet of sand," the Board reported, "sulphuretted [*sic*] hydrogen gas was encountered, which seriously affected the eyes of the workmen and caused some delay."

In July of 1897 work on the superstructure began. "The brickwork was finished on July 12, the copper roof and lantern gallery on July 13, the woodwork on July 23, the flashing and plumbing on July 27," the Board noted proudly, "and all the painting, hard oiling, etc., by August 5, when the light-house was accepted." Also during July, another 475 tons of granite riprap were placed around the foundation. Fortunately, the Fresnel lens had been saved from the wrecked lighthouse and could be reinstalled in the new caisson. "The light-house," the Board wrote in its 1898 annual report,

> *consists of a cast-iron foundation cylinder, filled with concrete, 30 feet
> in diameter and 45 feet in height, supporting an octagonal two-story
> brick dwelling, with a square tower rising 30 feet above the top of the
> cylinder. On this tower rests the lantern, which shows a light of the
> fourth-order flashing white every thirty seconds, with a red sector
> covering the shoals off Smith Point.*

The octagonal brick dwelling was painted white, the lantern black and the caisson foundation brown. The caisson and lighthouse, constructed from the same plans as Wolf Trap light, showed a French-cut Fresnel lens, 20 inches in diameter, with six panels, each of which contained a bull's-eye. Four iron columns supported the clock case for lens rotation and the lens. In 1936, the watch room contained the standby bell and bell striker which had been superseded by a diaphonic fog signal which was also located at the watch level on the east side of the tower. The inspector reported that it took 10 minutes to start the compressor for the signal and that the hand-bell was used in the interim. At that time, the lighthouse station had three boats—a twenty-two foot skiff, an eighteen-foot skiff, and a twenty-two foot motorboat. The nearest community was Sunnybank, four and one-half miles up the Little Wicomico River. By 1936, the station had also been outfitted with radio equipment.

In the early 1970's, off-shore electricity was supplied to the lighthouses and it was placed entirely on unmanned operation (submarine cables were run approximately three miles from a shoreline power service). In the 1980's, the cables needed replacement and, for a time, the Coast Guard considered deactivating the light station. Public outcry was fierce. "Damage to a submarine cable requires proper engineering—corrective action and preventive maintenance—not relocation of a properly located and essential aid to navigation," wrote one irate Chesapeake mariner. "The illogic is incomprehensible." In 1988, new submarine power cable was installed.

The cantilevered privy was a feature of both screwpile and caisson lights. Along with the wrought-iron balustrade, the Smith Point privy was given a fresh coat of paint by maintenance crews in 1988. Photo, U.S. Coast Guard.

From July, 22, 1991 until August 1 of the same year, maintenance crews aboard the Coast Guard Tender Gentian worked on a major overhaul of the lighthouse. A barge was also secured to the light that held special heavy equipment such as a crane and manlift. The crew power-washed the exterior of the lighthouse from the roof to the water line and scraped away remaining loose paint with wire brushes. Cracks in the brickwork were mortared and all the brickwork was painted with latex paint. Bad sections of the handrails on the upper gallery deck were replaced and the entire balustrade was sandblasted, primed and painted. Sealant was applied to the roof. The interior of the lighthouse was scraped and painted, the windows were replaced with vented acrylic panels and the window trim was painted green, "as found," the commanding officer of the Gentian reported, "when [the] plywood was removed." The outhouse was thoroughly refurbished, the old foghorn was removed and a "nonhistoric lifting support" was removed from the entranceway.

The commanding officer provided a detailed list of the renovation as well as a list of additional work items that he hoped could be undertaken. He expressed great pride in the work accomplished: "Smith Point has undergone a dramatic transformation."

Wolf Trap

On March 3, 1819 the Secretary of the Treasury received an appropriation from Congress "for building a light-house on Windmill Point, at the south of the Rappahannock River, or a light vessel or boat-on Wolf Trap Shoals, if the latter shall be deemed preferable to a light-house on Windmill Point...." Evidently, the shoal light was found to be of greater need, and two years later, in 1821, the brand new 180-ton Wolf Trap light vessel, carrying two fixed lights visible for 10 miles (one at an elevation of 30 feet and the other at 38 feet) and a fog bell, was established on the shoal. The vessel was painted a lead-gray color and the name Wolf Trap was lettered in black on either side of the "floating light."

According to an article that appeared in the April 1951 edition of *Chesapeake Skipper*, the shoal acquired its name during the colonial period when a 350-ton vessel, "Their Majesties Hyred Ship Wolfe," captained by George Purvis, was enlisted by the Royal Navy to curtail piracy and smuggling, and "to enforce the detested Navigation Acts."

As radio signaling and receiving equipment were added to lighthouses, they looked more and more like the creations of a science fiction set designer. In 1964 veteran civilian Lighthouse Service keeper Floyd Earl Crewe had two diesel generators to furnish electricity and enjoyed both air conditioning and television. Photo, U.S. Coast Guard.

Some time during 1691 the Wolfe had the misfortune to run aground on the shoal to which she was reluctantly to bestow her name. In this exposed situation in the middle of the Chesapeake, Purvis sensibly lost no time in summoning aid. Watermen of Middlesex and Gloucester Counties...rose to the occasion and so willingly and well did all hands turn to, that in a comparatively short time the Wolfe was relieved of guns, ammunition and stores, pumped out and dragged clear of the shoal with apparently negligible damage. Purvis was free to admit that without help the Wolfe would have been "utterly lost."

But in spite of the assistance so speedily and effectively provided by the watermen, Purvis refused payment. Angered, the watermen petitioned the colonial governor for redress, and he responded with a proclamation holding Captain Purvis accountable to "the salvors of H.M.S. Wolfe" and directing the Lords of Trade and Plantations to garnish his wages. In the end, the owners of the ship offered security for Captain Purvis's obligations. Though the claims were shortly resolved, the events were somewhat cynically remembered by the local watermen and hence the shoal was thereafter called Wolf Trap.

When, in the mid 19th century, the Light-House Board assumed responsibility for the country's aids to navigation, it voiced displeasure with the condition of many lightships in the Chesapeake Bay. In August of 1854 the Wolf Trap light vessel was removed from its station for repair and refitting. The Light-House Board reported that the boat was "towed to Alexandria, Virginia, all work having been suspended at Norfolk and Portsmouth in consequence of the yellow fever at those places." The vessel was completely repaired, recaulked and outfitted with new lanterns and lights and remained in service until it was destroyed during the Civil War. The 1862 report of the Light-House Board notes, "All the light-vessels from Cape Henry southward...and those in Chesapeake Bay (except Hooper's Straits and Jane's Is-

Starke Jett

land), have been removed and sunk or destroyed by the insurgents." The Wolf Trap light vessel was destroyed in 1861.

Although another light vessel was placed at Wolf Trap in 1864, the Light-House Board had become thoroughly enamored with the screwpile lighthouse even before the outbreak of the Civil War. Clearly, construction costs, maintenance and personnel requirements made it a much more cost-effective maritime light. "Whenever any of the light vessels occupying positions which are adapted to the erection of light-houses upon pile-foundations require to be rebuilt," the Light-House Board stated in 1859, "or require such extensive repairs as to render the substitution of such light-houses advisable and practicable, such permanent structures may be erected in place of any such light-vessels..." In the spring of 1870, two schooners carried the ironwork and

Wolf Trap was equipped with a diaphone and radio beacon. It was operated as a distance finding station—an important aid to navigators in fixing their position on the bay. A signal was transmitted on the fifth minute of every six-minute period. Three precision clocks ensured the correct timing of the transmission. Photo, U.S. Coast Guard.

the clapboard hexagonal lighthouse dwelling (which had been built at the Lazaretto Depot in Baltimore) to the site, marked by buoys, that had been selected for Wolf Trap light. The substratum was found to be extremely firm and the Light-House Board felt confident that the lighthouse could withstand severe storms and moving ice (and, in fact, the lighthouse did survive for almost 25 years). Unlike the solid cast-iron piles later used in the foundations of Drum Point and Hooper Strait, the lighthouse was built on a foundation of wooden pilings covered with cast-iron screw sleeves.

Construction was interrupted when the workmen's platform was carried away in a gale and thus the fourth-order light was not exhibited to mariners until October 1, 1870. The light was fixed white, varied by a white flash every 30 seconds. Built in 16 feet of water, the focal plane of the light was 38 feet and was visible for 11 nautical miles. The superstructure was painted in the same lead color as the light vessel and a red sector was added to mark the shoals.

In January of 1893, heavy ice floes severed the lighthouse from its foundation and it was carried 20 miles south where it was found by a cutter a few days later. It was still floating—though only its roof and lantern remained visible above the water—about one mile northeast of Thimble Shoal, heading towards the Virginia Capes. The keeper, John William Thomas of New Point, Virginia, escaped shortly before the lighthouse was swept away and was able to walk over the ice to a nearby tugboat trapped in the frozen waters of the Chesapeake Bay. The illuminating apparatus and some other items were salvaged from the floating wreck before the lighthouse was towed to shore and these were sent to the Portsmouth depot for storage.

Shortly after the incident, the lighthouse tender Holly was moored on Wolf Trap shoal to serve as a light vessel until July of 1893 when light vessel No. 46 could be put into service. Meanwhile, steps were taken by the Light-House Board to replace the screwpile structure with a caisson light. ("It was determined to replace it by a structure which could withstand such attacks [of ice], by means of its inherent weight and solidity," the Board noted in its annual report.) Proposals were requested in July of 1893 and contracts for the iron-work and wooden caisson were signed in August. Although the caisson was finished in November, the Light-House Board reported that "it was not until late in December that there was a tide sufficiently high to permit its being launched." The report continues,

> *The lower sections of the iron cylinder were then placed on the caisson, and on January 13, 1894, these parts of the structure were towed to the site. The caisson was not grounded on its site until nearly a week later on account of rough weather experienced on the way down the bay. On February 29, 1894, the air lock and pneumatic machinery were put in, and on March 5, 1894, the sinking of the structure commenced. In two weeks the required depth was reached and the filling of the caisson with concrete was completed.*

In April the foundation was completed and the fourth-order light, visible for 11 miles, was lit on September 20, 1894. The focal plane of the light is 52 feet.

The dwelling is a two-story octagonal brick building (each side is eight feet long), essentially identical to the lighthouse at Smith Point, with a square tower which provides a third-story watch room, eight-by-eight-feet square, supporting the lantern and lantern deck. Sometime in the late 1920's or early 1930's the exterior brick of the dwelling was painted red to protect the brick from damage caused by freezing salt water spray. Because of its radio calibration station, Wolf Trap light was one of the last to be manned on the Chesapeake Bay and it remained in excellent condition until it was fully automated in 1971. Thereafter, the inevitable process of deterioration began.

In 1991 a service team on the U.S. Coast Guard Tender Cowslip water-blasted, scraped and repainted the exterior of the light, scraped the interior paint, replaced the window panes with ventilated acrylic panels (the lantern panes remain glass to allow a truer reflection of the light), retarred the roof, and performed other general maintenance. Finally, the light was removed from the peak of the cupola where it had been placed some years before and returned to the interior pedestal of the lantern. In fact, two lanterns had been placed on top of the cupola. D.S. LaPierre, the officer in charge of the Coast Guard Aids to Navigation Team at Milford Haven formally requested that the light be returned to the lantern in April of 1991. "Personnel must climb up onto the top of the cupola, and are limited to only one square foot of area in which to stand," he informed the commander of the Fifth District.

> *After arranging themselves in this precarious position they then must lean out and tend to the task of servicing not one but two 300mm lanterns. In a nutshell this setup is both unsafe to service and, given that we are maintaining an entire lighthouse with a perfectly good gallery in which to mount a light...it is certainly unnecessary.*

Wolf Trap remains a familiar day mark and an active light, important to mariners on the Chesapeake Bay.

Light station established:
1821

Construction of present structure:
1894

Location:
In 16 feet of water, on the east end of Wolf Trap Spit, Virginia, west side of the Chesapeake Bay.

Position:
37 23 25
76 11 23

Characteristic of light:
Flashing white, 15-second interval.

Height of light, above mean high water:
52 feet.

Range:
11 miles.

Description of station:
Brown cylindrical foundation pier expanding in trumpet shape at its upper end to form a gallery, surmounted by an octagonal red-brick dwelling with a square tower; black lantern.

New Point Comfort

In two separate acts on March 3, 1801, Congress appropriated a total of $8,500 for construction of a Chesapeake Bay light at New Point Comfort to mark the north side of the entrance to Mobjack Bay and the York River. The lighthouse was constructed by Elzy Burroughs—who also built the light at Old Point Comfort and who, incidentally, was appointed in 1804 by then-president Thomas Jefferson as the first keeper of the New Point Comfort light station. The structure, an octagonal sandstone tower, was painted and whitewashed, inside and out, and stood 58 feet above mean high water. When outfitted with a Fresnel lens in 1865, its fourth-order fixed white light was visible for 13 miles.

New Point Comfort is the third-oldest lighthouse on the Chesapeake Bay (the two older lights are Old Cape Henry and Old Point Comfort). In 1852, the newly formed Light-House Board found the light in "passable" condition overall though its upkeep was wanting in several important respects and these were explained in detail by the Board's inspector. The keeper, who received a salary of $400 per year, "kept a negro woman of his own," the report states (giving one to assume that she was a slave), as his assistant. She received no salary. The keeper managed the light according to his own estimation of what needed to be done. For example, he believed that his light "was not considered bad in the bay," though he clearly had his own ideas about when the light should be lit—at dark, rather than at sunset as was specified in his written instructions—and he saw no need for curtains to protect the illuminating apparatus during daylight hours. The keeper also reported that he kept no watch since he always awoke "at the right time." The Light-House Board inspector found the reflectors scratched and in need of both silvering and cleaning and the burners in

New Point Comfort in the late 19th century. The light station was situated on a remote but lovely beach. A 1933 hurricane separated New Point Comfort from the mainland. Photo, The National Archives.

poor repair. The tone of the report makes clear that this was just the sort of lighthouse keeping that the new Light-House Board intended to correct with the utmost speed. "The light," the Board's inspector reported, "should illuminate the whole horizon."

The 1865 report of the Light-House Board mentioned that extensive repairs were needed at the light station and in 1868 these were completed. Throughout the late 19th century, the lighthouse and its comfortable frame dwelling were upgraded and well cared for. In 1882, for example, a new back

Starke Jett

Light station established:
1804

Construction of present structure:
1804

Location:
On New Point Comfort, Virginia (now just a tiny rocky outcropping separated from the mainland), north side of the entrance to Mobjack Bay, west side of the Chesapeake Bay.

Position:
37 18 04
76 16 41

Characteristic of light:
Inactive.

Height of light, above mean high water:
58 feet.

Description of station:
White stone tower.

porch was added to the dwelling and the front porch was repaired. The station was frequently painted and, in 1900, 184 feet of rail fence and plank walkways were installed around the lighthouse and dwelling. But times were changing, and when, in 1919, the light was partially automated, the keeper's house was torn down and the keeper, perhaps not surprisingly, quit the service altogether. A local resident of Mathews County was appointed to look after the lighthouse tower. It was completely automated in 1930.

Since 1933, when a major hurricane brought tidal floods to the western shores of the Chesapeake Bay, the lighthouse has been separated from the mainland. In the early part of the century, New Point Beach gained fame as a lovely bathing and camping spot, a popular, if remote, location for weekend outings and a favorite destination for yachting parties. After the hurricane, when the beach was separated from the mainland, the island had eroded so rapidly that today New Point light stands alone on a rocky outcropping so small as to hardly qualify as an island. In 1963, when a fully automated beacon was placed 1,050 yards offshore, the light was officially classified as a day marker. Five years later the U.S. Coast Guard discontinued all maintenance and effectively abandoned the station.

In 1972 local citizens succeeded in having the structure placed on the register of the Virginia Historic Landmarks Commission and thereafter community interest in preservation of the structure grew. The lighthouse was deeded to Mathews County in 1975 and the following year the Mathews County Board of Supervisors established the New Point Lighthouse Committee. At this time, the old tower was in extremely poor repair, from the top of the lantern to its very foundation, and increasingly threatened by the rapid erosion of the island. The windows, doors and all the glass panes of the lantern were gone. Birds used the tower as a nesting site and shelter. To make matters worse, the nearest safe landing was over a mile from the lighthouse tower, making the task of repairing the lighthouse difficult.

The newly formed New Point Lighthouse Committee immediately set about the work of raising money and stabilizing the structure and the communities of Mathews and Gloucester Counties, Virginia, pitched in. Funds were sought from state and federal agencies. By September 1978, with monies collected from private individuals, organizations, businesses and the Virginia Landmarks Commission, they had succeeded in making some initial repairs to the brickwork, repairing and painting the iron lantern, installing a new ladder from the top of the tower to the lantern deck and constructing a dock on the island. Meanwhile, a study was underway by the Virginia Institute of Marine Science to ascertain the long range effects of erosion around the island.

In 1981 and 1988, major renovations of the New Point lighthouse were completed. In 1981, approximately $80,000 in structural repairs was funded by the community, the State of Virginia and the J. Edwin Treakle Foundation. Once again, in 1988, approximately $24,000—a $10,000 federal grant and $14,000 raised locally—was spent in repairs to the dock and to replace windows and shutters. One of the provisions of the restoration grant provided by the federal government was a stipulation that the lighthouse remain open to the public, and thus the decision was made to keep the key to the lighthouse in the county's planning and zoning office in Mathews where it could be checked out by persons wishing to visit the tower. In spite of a careful registration process, lighthouse keys began to disappear and numerous instances of trespassing and destruction of lighthouse property were reported. Sadly, vandalism has now become the most serious threat to preservation of this historic Chesapeake Bay structure. In 1994, vandals removed the lock on the door to the tower, windows were smashed, shutters were torn from their hinges, and graffiti once again adorned the inside of the tower and lantern. The key has now been turned over to the county administrator's office, but acts of vandalism continue. Because there is no electricity on the premises, electronic surveillance is not a feasible solution. The sheriff's office in Mathews believes that the only way to keep people away from the lighthouse is make it off-limits to everyone, to patrol it, and to arrest anyone caught trespassing.

In 1919, the New Point Comfort light station was partially automated and the charming keeper's house was torn down. In 1930 the tower was completely automated and in 1963 the lighthouse was replaced with an offshore beacon. Photo (c. 1930), U.S. Coast Guard.

Thimble Shoal

Like Wolf Trap light, the Thimble Shoal lighthouse was built (in accordance with the 1859 regulations of the Light-House Board) to replace a light vessel that had been active at Willoughby's Spit in the early years of the 19th century. Willoughby's Spit and "The Thimble" entrance to Hampton Roads were parallel bars which constituted a danger to large vessels entering Hampton Roads. For many years, light vessels were used to mark the channel between them, but in 1870 an appropriation was made to substitute a permanent lighthouse. "It is believed..." the Light-House Board wrote in its annual report, "that the same end may be attained at much less annual expense by the erection of an iron screw-pile light-house on The Thimble of Horseshoe Bar..."

In 1871 the Light-House Board was still enthusiastic about screwpile construction, though it was recognized that the position of the Thimble Shoal lighthouse was "very exposed, particularly to strong easterly winds." Thus, the Board suggested a screwpile foundation of "more than ordinary strength." "It will be advisable, also," the Board continued, "to protect the site and give more stability to the foundation by throwing in about it loose stones to a depth of about three feet."

In August of 1871, a contract was accepted but construction was delayed until the following spring. "As was anticipated," the Board reported,

Distinguished by its porthole windows and its circular lantern with curved diamond shaped storm panels, the Thimble Shoal caisson was constructed in 1914 to replace a screwpile destroyed when it was rammed by a schooner. Photo (c. 1930), U.S. Coast Guard.

> *the shoal proved to be very hard, consisting of fine compact sand, which rendered the process of screwing in the piles very slow. Further delay was experienced by the breaking of a cast-iron column used as a follower on the pile...and also by the breaking of one of the screws, owing to a defective casting.*

On October 15, the fixed white light, varied by red and white flashes, was exhibited for the first time and the lightship on the opposite side of the channel was withdrawn. "This light-house," the Board noted, "replaces the last light-ship in this district." Three and one-half miles from Old Point Comfort light, the screwpile was built in 11 feet of water; the lantern, foundation and roof of the hexagonal cottage were painted brown—the house was drab (like the lightship that it replaced).

On October 30, 1880, the lighthouse was destroyed by a fire, the origin of which, the Board reported, had not been "definitely ascertained." Because of the importance of the light, however, it was necessary to begin reconstruction at once. "The iron-work," the Board wrote, "with slight exceptions, was found to be intact; the water-tanks, boat-davits, and part of the lanterns and lens were recovered by the aid of a diver." A new lighthouse had just been completed at the Lazaretto depot and it was decided to appropriate the new house (intended for Bell's Rock, Virginia) for use at Thimble Shoal. "On December 6," the Board continued,

> *the tender Tulip, with the necessary material and a working party on board, proceeded to the site and commenced the work of rebuilding. Though this work was delayed by severe storms, ice, and extremely cold*

Starke Jett

weather, the lens was in place and the light re-exhibited on December 24, having been extinguished only fifty-five days.

The focal plane of the fourth-order fixed light was 42½ feet, visible for almost 12 miles. Two fog bells were simultaneously struck by machinery every five seconds.

Once again, in March of 1891, the hexagonal screwpile lighthouse was "considerably damaged" when it was rammed by "an unknown steamer." Then in April of 1898, the unfortunate lighthouse was rammed by a coal barge.

The entire lower gallery on the southeast side was carried away and the two adjoining sides were damaged. All the joists in the southeast section were broken and thrust out of position. The lower socket casting on the south-by-east corner was badly cracked, and the 5-inch horizontal brace on the southeast side was bent about five inches out of line. Other parts of the ironworks suffered, and the house was lifted about one-half inch off the radial beams.

In fact, disaster struck Thimble Shoal at regular intervals until, finally, in December 1909, the hexagonal cottage was completely destroyed by fire and its pile foundation irreparably damaged after being rammed by the schooner Malcolm Baxter, Jr. The ship had just entered the bay from stormy Atlantic seas and was in tow by the John Twohy. Snow flurries and gale-force winds made the passage through the Thimble Shoal channel difficult. The Baxter pitched and pulled against the tow line, finally heading off from the tug when its steering mechanism failed. The Baxter's captain quickly relayed this information to the tug, but it was too late: the tug's crew had already cast off the tow line. Although the tug rushed back to try to make fast another line, they were not able to prevent the collision. Inside the lighthouse, two frightened keepers felt the impact and scrambled for their small craft as the floor gave way and their wood-stove turned over spilling hot coals which immediately ignited and turned the lighthouse into a raging inferno. As the small boat containing the two keepers bobbed helplessly in the angry sea, the Baxter continued to ram the lighthouse and the crew worked frantically to free the vessel before it, too, caught fire. Fortunately, the wind and waves forced the Baxter beyond the lighthouse, the crew of the Twohy rescued the keepers, and was successful in once again securing the vessel.

Although Congress acted quickly to appropriate funds for the construction of a new lighthouse, it was five years before the new structure was completed. Not surprisingly, the new light, a three-story, cast-iron tower, was built on a caisson foundation. The light is situated in one and three-quarter fathoms of water on the shoal off the Horseshoe on the northern side of the channel, only a few feet from the few remaining iron pilings of the original screwpile structure which, twisted and corroded, are still visible at low tide.

Standing 55 feet above the water line, Thimble Shoal is architecturally distinguished by its unusual porthole windows and its circular lantern, attractively fitted with curved panes in a diamond pattern. It is the only Chesapeake Bay lighthouse of the caisson type which still has its first-level gallery roof.

According to a 1938 inspection report, the seven-foot diameter lantern is constructed of cast iron with a steel lining and brass strips. The roof is also cast iron with a sheet-zinc lining and a cast-iron ventilator ball at its apex. The lightning conductor is bronze with a platinum tip, and the cupola gallery balustrade is made of steel and has a cast-iron deck. The lantern door is cast iron with a steel lining and brass hinges, as is the watchroom door into the lantern. There are four ventilators in the parapet walls. Originally, the fourth-order light contained a lens manufactured in Paris by Barbier, Benard and Turenne. The diameter of the lens was $19^{1}/_{2}$ inches and the light was occulting—one second light, one second dark—with eclipses produced by an opaque panel. The rotating mechanism was protected by a glass case in a brass frame. Four two-inch steel columns supported the clock case and lens. Although by 1938 a five-foot-long diaphone horn was in use as a fog signal, the bronze bell manufactured in Baltimore in 1900 was still kept as a backup for emergencies. Water was collected in concrete cisterns built into the lower level of the tower in the caisson foundation and, in the inspector's estimation, the water was of good quality and the station was "healthful."

Thimble Shoal light was automated in 1964. In 1986-87 a solar electric generator was installed to power the navigational aids on the lighthouse and the Coast Guard reported that the submarine power cable was "disestablished." (Actually, 80-pound lead-acid battery packs had provided the primary power source for over 20 years, but these were difficult—even dangerous—to get on board the light station.)

In 1988, extensive restoration work was carried out by the U.S. Coast Guard. In September, the tender Red Cedar and a 100-foot barge dropped anchor next to Thimble Shoal—one of seven Chesapeake Bay lighthouses slated for extensive restoration that year— and though of fairly recent construction, the lighthouse judged most badly in need of repair because of its exposed location. "The idea," Coast Guard Engineering Officer Larry Ames explained, "is to make it look right—to maintain its historical integrity."

An inspection carried out in December of 1993 indicated that further work needed to be done. The inspection team found that a portion of the main concrete deck was missing and that the main-level decking contained numerous small cracks. Flaking, peeling and running rust were observed in both the interior and exterior paint surface and the Coast Guard inspection team recommended repainting the entire structure with a paint compatible with the underlying vinyl coating applied to the lighthouse in 1988. They also urged that the lighthouse be painted in its former red color. The historically accurate brownish-red shade of the caisson applied in 1988 did not, they believed, provide adequate "mariner discernment." The team also noted that discolored acrylic glazing was hampering the light's effectiveness and recommended that the lantern panes be replaced with ultraviolet stabilized acrylic panes. Finally, they once again recommended removal of the remaining debris—the so-called "derelict steel foundation"—of the wrecked screwpile.

Thimble Shoal remains an active light of critical importance to ships moving in and out of the Norfolk and Hampton Roads area— still one of the most heavily navigated channels in the world.

The Building of
Thimble Shoal

The previous lighthouse at Thimble Shoal was destroyed by fire in 1909.

When the ironwork of the new 1914 lighthouse was completed, it was sent to the buoy depot (probably Portsmouth) where the part of the caisson foundation that was to be sunk into the bay was floated behind a barge to the lighthouse site. The lowest course of plates is the broadest.

The next step was to sink the caisson at the chosen site. Great care was taken to ensure that the lighthouse did not tilt. Sometimes derricks were required to keep the lighthouse on the perpendicular.

In soft, muddy parts of the bay, the caisson would sink of its own accord, but at Thimble Shoal hard compact sand meant that both dredging equipment and a heavy rock and concrete filling were needed to help ground the substructure.

All photos (c 1914) National Archives.

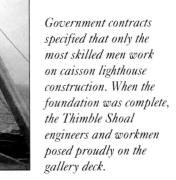

Government contracts specified that only the most skilled men work on caisson lighthouse construction. When the foundation was complete, the Thimble Shoal engineers and workmen posed proudly on the gallery deck.

Note that the top tier (at Thimble Shoal, the seventh course of plates) again flares out to create a larger surface for the tower and surrounding gallery deck.

Once the caisson was grounded, completion of the light-house was generally fairly rapid. At Thimble Shoal the iron pilings of the wrecked screwpile afforded a good foundation for the workmen's quarters and equipment.

Old Point Comfort

The second oldest light on the Chesapeake Bay, Old Point Comfort was commissioned in 1802, four years after Congress had approved construction of the lighthouse. Located directly in front of Fort Monroe, at the entrance to Hampton Roads, the Old Point Comfort lighthouse was not, however, the first navigational aid to be employed on that site. Fortifications had existed at the point in colonial days; Fort George preceded Fort Monroe and was probably preceded by another fortification. It has even been suggested that Indians used wood fires on the point to act as navigational aids for Spanish ships during the 16th century. However, it is conclusively known that in 1775 a man named John Dams, a former caretaker of the ruins at Fort George, received the sum of 20 pounds annually for showing a light there.

In 1798, an act of the Virginia legislature authorized the governor to convey land at Old Point Comfort to the federal government for the construction of a lighthouse. The following year the land was surveyed and, in 1800, Congress appropriated $1500 to begin construction. One year later, another $3500 was added to the original appropriation. The contractor, Elzy Burroughs (who also built the light at New Point Comfort), completed most of the work on the octagonal stone tower in 1803. Four large windows afford light to the spiral stone steps that lead to the iron ladder and trap door that is the entrance to the lens chamber. Before being outfitted with a Fresnel lens, the signal required eleven oil lanterns (consuming 486 gallons of oil annually) and a like number of fourteen-inch reflectors. The signal was visible for fourteen miles on a clear day. The tower was whitewashed, inside and out, every two years.

When British forces sailed into the Chesapeake Bay during the War of 1812, notice was given that the lighthouses of the Chesapeake Bay were to be extinguished. Norfolk was successfully defended against British attack, but the Jack Tars and Royal Marines (under Rear Admiral George Cockburn) attacked, captured, and later burned Hampton. Part of their force moved to Old Point Comfort where the lighthouse was used as an observation post.

At the end of the war, the construction of Fort Monroe and the construction of several hotels that catered to the area's growing popularity as a resort began to turn Old Point Comfort into a busy place. In 1854, $6,000 was appropriated for erection of a fog bell tower which was completed the following year. The bronze bell, 40 inches in diameter and 36 inches in height, was audible for three miles. An additional beacon-light was added shortly thereafter, apparently to mark the entrance for anchorage at Fort Monroe. This light was discontinued in 1869, but the main light remained active.

Because of the military presence and because of the area's popularity with vacationers, the Old Point Comfort lighthouse received a great deal of public attention and, though it is one of the oldest lighthouses on the Chesapeake Bay, it has been kept in superb condition. In 1891, a new keeper's dwelling was constructed. "The dwelling," the Light-House Board reported, "which was very old and beyond economical repair, was rebuilt; new outbuildings,

Commissioned in 1802, Old Point Comfort was not fully automated until 1973. The stone tower is located on Fort Monroe. Still in excellent condition, Old Point Comfort light remains an active navigational aid. Photo, U.S. Coast Guard.

Starke Jet

Light station established:
1802

Construction of
present structure:
1802

Location:
On the north side of the
entrance to Hampton Roads,
Virginia, on the beach directly
in front of Fort Monroe.

Position:
37 00 06
76 14 24

Characteristic of light:
Flashing (2) red, 12-second
interval; white sector 2-second
flash, 2-second eclipse; white
sector from 265 to 038 degrees.
Emergency light of reduced
intensity displayed when main
light is inoperative.

Height of light, above
mean high water:
54 feet.

Range:
White, 16 miles; red, 14 miles.

Description of station:
Octagonal cut-stone tower,
painted white; black lantern;
white keeper's dwelling.

including a stable, 25 feet by 14 feet in plan, were constructed; 270 lineal feet of iron and 420 lineal feet of wooden fencing were put up; the tower was scraped, pointed, and painted, and other minor repairs were made." In 1901, after sewer pipe had been laid to the lighthouse, the dug-up area, under the daily scrutiny of travelers, seaside tourists and officers, required landscaping and the Light-House Board proudly noted the provision of plants, flower seeds, a lawnmower, and 150 feet of garden hose for "improving the grounds."

The 20th century brought numerous additional changes as manned flight and increasing use of electricity suggested new ways of managing the light and fog signal. First of all, incandescent electric lights were installed in the fourth-order lens. At one time, the roof was painted with a pattern to assist in aerial navigation, marking the path from Norfolk to Washington, D.C. For a time, beginning in 1936, a light beam flashed from Fort Wool was used to automatically start and stop the fog signal at Old Point Comfort. When the beam—emitted at two-minute intervals onto a photoelectric cell at the light station—was disrupted, the fog warning was automatically switched on. Similarly, when visibility improved, it would turn off. The strangest, at least in appearance, of these experiments was the addition of spokes from the cat-walk, each of which showed a 250-watt bulb. Keeper William J. Clark obtained permission in the 1950's to create this strange apparition so that the lighthouse would retain its distinctiveness in competition with growing numbers of lights along the coastline.

The station was not automated until January of 1973, and, until that time, two keepers and their families occupied the lighthouse dwelling. Over the years, the characteristics of the light have been changed several times, though usually some combination of white and red has been shown. In 1905, for example, the Board reported that "the light was again changed to fixed red through the entire arc of visibility." In the 1950's the ruby glass still remained inside the storm panes but today the automated light shows a flashing signal, only 138 degrees of which is white.

Phyllis Sprock, an Army ecologist, made a detailed inventory of the historic lighthouse tower and keeper's dwelling in 1980 and, likewise, recent U.S. Coast Guard inspection and maintenance reports carefully enumerate the condition of the tower's exterior and interior. One surmises that the Old Point Comfort light station is a point of pride for both the U.S. Coast Guard and the U.S. Army at Fort Monroe.

The octagonal cut-stone lighthouse tower has wood double-hung windows (four panes over four panes) and a solid steel door with a sign denoting the lighthouse as a Virginia National Landmark. The door and window trim are a narrow cove-and-bead molding. Just under the lantern deck there is an exterior cornice molding, visible in photographs. The tower floor is brick and the steps to the landing are cut stone, smoothed and squared on top and in front, and rough-cut underneath. The treads circle a stone column leading to the top of the tower. Because the interior walls were originally whitewashed, Sprock found that lime had combined with water to form calcium carbonate, "a coating," she wrote,

> that is sometimes known as 'cave varnish.' Algae are feeding on this; [nevertheless] the formation of $CaCo_3$ and the algal covering are

The circular bell-shaped roof of the octagonal lantern is copper, painted a dull red in 1980, and topped with a large ventilator ball and lightning rod. The lantern gallery is accessible through a wooden half-door and is surrounded by a wrought-iron railing. The emergency light is mounted on top of a metal rod and is turned on automatically if there is any interruption in the commercial power which the lighthouse uses.

The prisms of the light's fourth-order Fresnel lens cover approximately three-quarters of the arc of the lantern ("the other quarter," Sprock mused, "being the north side, where landlubbers seldom need navigational aids").

Studying early maps of the site, Sprock deduced that there was no separate keeper's dwelling until 1823—only a tiny oilhouse identified on an 1820 map. The building marked "keeper" appears on an 1823 map but not at the spot of the present dwelling. The present house, Sprock noted, "exhibits influences from the Shingle Style of the 1870's, the Stick Style of the 1860's and 1870's, a touch of Queene Anne, and a soupçon of Eastlake." In the 1970's, when the beacon was automated, the Army acquired the property, made some changes to the interior, and leased the quarters.

The frame house has elaborately trimmed gables and unusual double-hung windows, most of them 12 over two panes. The door and window trim is plain and a simple molding adorns the eaves beneath the gables. The roof is gray asphalt shingle; the semi-octagonal porch has an eight-sided roof that rises to a point. Sprock found the duplex keeper's quarters in very good condition, though most of the original interior doors had been removed.

In 1989, the Coast Guard personnel scraped the loose paint from the masonry interior of the lighthouse tower to help the walls "breathe." A worklist was also generated for 1990 maintenance. At this time the interior was apparently pressure washed to remove algae and painted (though painting had been specifically ruled out as offering any benefit by both the Army ecologist and the 1989 Coast Guard inspection team), the tower light was replaced, windows that had been painted shut were freed, the lantern ladder was primed and painted, the wood framing around the catwalk deck was replaced, the lantern panes were recaulked and broken panes replaced, the lantern pedestal was repainted—and so on. In 1994 the inspection team found "minor deficiencies" in need of correction. On the whole, however, the exterior stonework and mortar joints were found to be in good condition. Not so the interior masonry, however, where mortar joints between the stones were found to be crumbling. The Coast Guard recommended tuck-pointing the interior mortar joints and deteriorating stone. (This report curiously notes wood stairs to the lantern room whereas the 1989 inspection describes an iron ladder, corroded, in need of priming and painting, as does Sprock's 1980 report.) The inspection team found that the maintenance logs and wiring diagrams were not present.

Construction of the fog bell tower was authorized in 1854. The bronze bell, 36 inches high and 40 inches in diameter, was audible for three miles. This photo was taken in 1924. Photo, U.S. Coast Guard.

Newport News Middle Ground

In 1887, the Light-House Board recommended that Congress appropriate $50,000 for the construction of a lighthouse to mark the Middle Ground shoal in Hampton Roads. "An examination of the shoal in question, with reference to a foundation for a light-house," the Board noted, "shows that it is composed of sand and clay until, at 32 feet in depth below the surface of the bottom, perfectly clean white sand is reached. There is, therefore, no doubt about the suitability of the foundation." But, the Board surmised, the depth of the water posed construction difficulties ("17 feet of water at low tide or about 21 feet at high tide"), as did winter ice and heavy traffic in

Hampton Roads. "It will be exposed to shocks from fields of running ice, and being in comparatively deep water will also be exposed to the danger of being run into by both steam and sailing vessels. Under the circumstances," the Board wrote, "no structure less suitable than an iron caisson should be built."

In 1888, the necessary appropriation was made by Congress, and the following year the Light-House Board reported that "plans and specifications...are now being prepared." In November of 1889, requests for proposals were publicized, but the lowest bid was found to "leave too small a margin for the purchase of the materials to be supplied to the contractors by the Government and for incidental and contingent expenses." "Accordingly," the Board reported,

modifications, which would not impair its stability, were made in the substructure, the quantity of riprap stone was reduced one-third and the matter was then resubmitted to the lowest bidder for the erection of the light-house, with a request for a reduced offer...

When the contractor lowered his bid by $4,000 it was promptly accepted and work was begun.

The framing of the crib was commenced at Newport News, Virginia, about May 1, and it was completed by the middle of June. The iron caisson was delivered at the Portsmouth, Virginia, depot, and the cement required for the work was landed and is being stored there. The iron superstructure is nearly finished at the contractor's shops and will soon be inspected and shipped.

Construction of the lighthouse proceeded smoothly. "In July," the Board reported,

the wooden caisson with four sections of the dredging shaft and two courses of the foundation cylinder was towed to the site and sunk. .... By the end of October the fifth course of plates had been placed on the cylinder and the caisson had reached the depth designed—the stratum of clean, white sand 34 feet below the surface of the shoal.

The concrete and sand filling was deposited to within nine feet of the top, and, in December, erection of the iron tower which had been completed and delivered to the buoy depot in Portsmouth, was begun and was completed the following month. One thousand tons of riprap stone were placed around the base to protect it from the undermining action of currents and in March the lighthouse was "formally accepted." "On April 15,

Starke Jett

First commissioned in 1891, Newport News Middle Ground light was changed to unmanned operation in 1954 and it was downgraded to the status of a second-class tall nun buoy. Photo (c. 1950), U.S. Coast Guard.

115

1891," the Board stated, "the light was first exhibited from the lens for the benefit of mariners." The fourth-order lens showed a fixed white light, varied by a white flash every 20 seconds, visible for 12 miles.

The caisson foundation of Newport News Middle Ground light is 25 feet in diameter and 56 feet in height. The caisson, which is painted black, shows approximately 15 feet above the water. The brown conical tower is 29 feet in height with a 21-foot diameter base. The precise height of the light above mean high water is $51\frac{1}{2}$ feet (the Coast Guard generally rounds these numbers off in published light lists). The octagonal lantern is cast iron and the roof is tin. An iron pedestal supported the fourth-order lens and light. Originally the light was outfitted with a Stevens fog bell which was struck by machinery—a double blow every 15 seconds.

The dwelling was inhabited by a keeper and one assistant who shared the living space afforded by three rooms. In addition, there was a watch room and a basement where cisterns were placed to collect rainwater from the first-level gallery roof by means of gutters fitted with strainers and downspouts.

In 1954, Newport News Middle Ground was changed to unattended operation and, at that time, the characteristic of both the light and the bell were also changed. In its local notice to mariners, the Coast Guard reported that the light would henceforth show a flashing white 3,000-candlepower light, and that the fog bell would sound one stroke every 15 seconds, continuously from September 15 to June 1. At the same time, the direction calibration service was discontinued and the light was downgraded to a "second-class tall nun buoy." All unnecessary equipment was removed, including the station boats. Servicing of the lighthouse to recharge batteries was to be undertaken at nine-day intervals.

In 1982, the Coast Guard planned to make repairs to the lighthouse and sent an inspection team to evaluate its physical condition, "preparatory," they reported "to Operation Spruce Up." The lighthouse was beginning to show signs of serious deterioration. The boarding ladders were in need of repair and some of the balustrade was missing from the gallery deck. They found holes in the gallery roof and, most serious of all, they found that some of the first-level decking had been knocked out in a 1979 ship collision with the lighthouse, allowing water to enter the caisson foundation. In the cellar they found flaking paint and leaking porthole windows. The cisterns were full of water and they were unable to immediately determine whether this water came from the foundation or the roof. On the first, second and third levels, they found flaking paint, leaking windows and portholes, seagull eggs and guano. The watch room was missing one entire window and the doors to the gallery were jammed open. Additionally, they found that the roof was perforated with holes. In the lantern room they found more flaking paint and open doors. The condition was so discouraging that one member of the inspection team volunteered to remain at the light as caretaker and to undertake the refurbishment of the lighthouse himself if funds could be provided.

As planned, general repairs were made, and between 1986 and 1987 the light was solarized. In 1988, the Coast Guard again spent $14,400 in work on the lighthouse. According to their maintenance lists, the structure was sandblasted and painted, the railings were replaced, and a new access ladder was installed. Nevertheless, deterioration continued and in 1992 an inspection once again revealed serious problems with the foundation and the ironwork of the tower. Rust and corrosion were eating away at the iron plates and water was found in the caisson foundation.

A 1994 inspection found the lighthouse in "fair overall condition with some noticeable structural defects." The inspection team observed pitting rust along the foundation waterline and "considerable rust" along the seams of the iron plates. The access ladder was badly corroded—a danger, the report stated, to servicing personnel. They found that one of the exterior supports of the cantilevered main deck was missing, that the underside of the first-level deck was badly corroded, and that approximately 30 percent of the main-deck balustrade was missing or damaged. Cracks in the interior concrete of the caisson were visible in the basement and in the interior masonry lining they observed mortar cracks and spalled brick. Once again, the inspection team found that the lantern room door did not close, allowing birds access to the interior. Unfortunately, the list goes on—even the maintenance logs and wiring diagrams were missing from the lighthouse—but the report concludes with a number of specific recommendations which hopefully will be carried out in the near future and which include the following: moving the light, which is now on a pole exterior to the lantern and dangerous to service, back to the pedestal inside the lantern, replacing the lantern panes which are clouded and yellowed, installing a locking device on the main access door to prevent unauthorized entry, and replacing the steel plating placed over porthole windows with vented acrylic glazing to improve ventilation in the tower. The inspection team recommended that structural repairs to the caisson and main deck be contracted out.

Newport News Middle Ground was outfitted with a fourth-order Fresnel lens which originally showed a fixed white light. The characteristic of the light was changed to flashing white when the station was automated (and has since been changed to isophase white). Photo (c. 1950), U.S. Coast Guard.

Cape Henry, Old

The old Cape Henry lighthouse—the third oldest lighthouse still standing in the United States and the oldest on the Chesapeake Bay—has the distinction of being the first lighthouse erected under the auspices of the United States government. In fact, the same act of the First Session of Congress which created a federal lighthouse service specifically mandated the construction of a lighthouse at Cape Henry. The act, approved on August 7, 1789, placed responsibility for "the establishment and support of light-houses, beacons, buoys and public piers" under the Secretary of the Treasury. All existing aids to navigation were to be transferred to the federal government and it was the duty of the Secretary to contract "for rebuilding, repairing, supplying and manning" all light stations. A few days after passage, the bill was signed by George Washington and forwarded to Governor Beverly Randolph of Virginia. By March of 1790, appropriations had been approved for construction of the Cape Henry light.

The swiftness with which the federal government moved to establish the Cape Henry light station was in large part a response to 70 years of colonial ineptness—bureaucratic blundering and red tape—with respect to the Virginia assembly's oft-expressed need for a seaworthy beacon at the Cape. Although beacon fires were often used to aid mariners entering the Chesapeake Bay at night, pirates were also always on the watch for these opportunities.

The old Cape Henry light, visible in the background, is quite similar to the Cape Henlopen lighthouse built in 1767. Commissioned in 1791, it was the first lighthouse completed under the auspices of the United States government. Photo, U.S. Coast Guard.

They would capture the men in charge of the beacon and move it southward to bring ships aground where the wreckers were waiting. Between piracy and foul weather, the wreckage at the Cape continued to grow. On November 24, 1720, Governor Alexander Spotswood sent the first petition to the Virginia House of Burgesses proposing construction of a lighthouse. The Virginia House responded favorably with a resolve, "That a lighthouse be built and maintained at Cape Henry at the Charge of the Colony of Virginia, Provided the Province of Maryland will contribute...towards Building and ...maintaining the Same forever." The project was to be financed, in part, by duty on shipping, and thus required approval from the British government. Spotswood lost no time in approaching the Board of Trade in England. He pointed to the benefits of a seacoast light for trade with Maryland and Virginia, and noted that vessels approaching the Virginia Capes in bad weather were presently afraid to venture into the Chesapeake, "whereas," he continued, "if such a lighthouse were built ships might then boldly venture, there being water enough and a good channell within little more than a musquett shote of the place where this lighthouse may be placed."

British merchants proved unsympathetic, however, and Virginia enlisted only passive cooperation from Maryland. Again, in 1727 and in 1752, the Virginia assembly acted favorably on proposals to establish a light station at Cape Henry. In 1758, the British Board of Trade added their support to the project,

Starke Jett

119

noting that tobacco merchants believed "a Lighthouse there would be a Security to all Ships & their Cargoes," and "a publick benefit."

Finally, in 1772, the Maryland assembly responded favorably with reciprocal legislation and a group of "directors" was appointed and authorized to select a design and purchase the materials to begin construction. Workers' quarters and stables were constructed and over 4,000 tons of stone were brought to the site. By June of 1775, the funds provided were almost spent and the directors requested an additional 5,000 pounds to complete the work. Soon thereafter, the Revolution brought construction to a halt and the stone began to settle into drifts of sand. Some of it was eventually recovered and used in the foundation of the Cape Henry light.

In March of 1791, a contract, signed by Alexander Hamilton as Secretary of the Treasury, was made with John McComb, Jr. Construction Co. and directed them, "with all convenient speed," to "build and finish in a good and workman like manner a Light House of Stone, Faced with hewn or hammer dressed Stone..."

Construction of the Cape Henry light was begun in August of 1791 and proved difficult. Thomas Newton, who had been sent by Secretary Hamilton to oversee the construction of the light, informed the Secretary of these difficulties and spoke highly of McComb's work. "He is persevering and merits much for his industry, the drifting of the sand is truly vexatious, for in an instant there came down fifty cart loads at least, in the foundation after it was cleaned for laying the stone, which he bore with great patience and immediately set to work and removed it without a murmur as to the payment for the additional work..." The foundation had to be laid at 20 feet rather than 13, as specified in the design, ("[A]t the depth of thirteen there was nothing but loose sand," Newton wrote, "at twenty it appeared solid and firm to anything we had before seen, it far exceeded any ideas of mine and I think there will be no danger of its ever giving way.") An additional $2,500 was required to complete the construction. The beacon was lit for mariners in October of the following year.

The design of the Cape Henry lighthouse is essentially the same as that of the Cape Henlopen, Delaware lighthouse built in 1767—and, apparently, may well have been built following the plans drawn up by the colonial administration. The octagonal stone tower stands 92-feet high on the summit of a 56-foot dune, tapering from a diameter of 26 feet at its base to a diameter of 16 feet at the top. The foundation is made of aquia sandstone and the tower is rosy Rappahannock sandstone. In addition, a two-story keeper's dwelling and an underground oil vault ("for the storage & safe keeping of the Oil belonging to the said Light House," to be covered with a shed furnished with "eight strong Cedar Cisterns with Covers, each capable of containing two hundred gallons of Oil...") were constructed at the light station.

In 1798, Benjamin Latrobe visited Cape Henry and made two sketches of the lighthouse. "It is," he wrote, "a good solid building of Rappahannock freestone, but has the unpardonable fault of a wooden staircase, which being necessarily soaked with oil, exposes the light to the perpetual risk of destruction by fire." Latrobe also described the incessant movement of sand around the lighthouse and keeper's dwelling as "a perpetual whirl around it, which licks up the sand from the smooth surface of the timber, and heaps it around in the form of a basin. .... The sandy rim, while it protects the keeper from the storms, renders his habitation one of the dreariest abodes imaginable."

In 1835, a new dwelling was constructed for the keeper, and in 1841 the lantern was replaced and outfitted with 18 new lamps and 18 reflectors. In 1844, a 15-foot high wall was constructed around the base of the tower and the area was paved. In 1855, a fog bell tower was constructed and two years later the reflecting apparatus was replaced with a second-order Fresnel lens. Also in 1857, the tower was lined in brick. The Civil War temporarily put the lighthouse out of commission. According to John B. Drew, the 17-year-old assistant keeper at the time, the tower was seized by men from Princess Anne County in April 1861, and the lamps and the lens were destroyed. Placed under military guard, it was repaired and back in operation in 1863. Meanwhile, a lightship was put into service at the entrance to the Chesapeake Bay.

In 1864, a Light-House Board inspector noted that "[t]he fine cut-stone tower at Cape Henry... is liable to injury from fire, in consequence of having an old-fashioned wooden stairway, greatly decayed and insecure. It is deemed advisable to provide a cast-iron spiral stairway for this tower..." The stairway was replaced and the station remained in good condition for another eight years.

Beginning in 1872, however, the Light-House Board noted "large cracks or openings, extending from the base upward," on six of the eight outside masonry walls. "Four of them," the Board continued, "are apparently less dangerous than the other two, and alone would not warrant any great apprehension of danger, but the latter, *viz*, those on the north and south faces, where the strength of the masonry is lessened by openings for windows, are very bad, extending from the base almost to the top of the tower." The Board concluded,

> *[T]he tower is in an unsafe condition...and a new one must be built. This old tower has done good service, ...but it has seen its best days, and now, from age and perhaps defective workmanship, it is in danger of being thrown down by some heavy gale.*

An appropriation was asked for to begin work on a new tower and $75,000 was finally granted in June 1878.

Somewhat to the surprise of everyone, the old Cape Henry lighthouse has neither crumbled nor been swept away in a storm. Though funds for its preservation have been scarce, it has proven of the greatest importance that the lighthouse was adopted early on by The Association for the Preservation of Virginia Antiquities. On April 29, 1896, officers and members of the association placed a tablet on the lighthouse marking "the first landing of the English colonists on Virginia's soil..." and thereafter the association membership remained interested in its preservation. In 1930 the lighthouse—along with 1.77 acres of ground—was transferred to The Association for the Preservation of Virginia Antiquities. In 1939, it was the site chosen for ceremonies commemorating the sesquicentennial of the Lighthouse Service—the same year, ironically, that maintenance was transferred to the U.S. Coast Guard.

Cape Henry, New

In its annual report of 1879, the Light-House Board noted that "drawings and specifications for a new 1st-order light-house are now completed and ready for distribution to bidders." The Board also reported that it was negotiating the purchase of six acres of land. "No unnecessary delay will be made in the prosecution of this important work," the Board continued. "Proposals for the metal-work will at once be carried on by day's labor." The Board asked for appropriation of an additional $25,000.

In 1880, the Light-House Board reported that construction was "fairly under way," although there had been some delays on all fronts—including the completion of the metal work, the on-site construction, and the land purchase negotiations. "At this date," the Board reported,

the cast-iron work of the entire structure is out of the sand, and about one-third of the wrought-iron work has been completed. The base section, comprising about 16 feet in height of the tower, is nearly completed. It was impracticable to commence operations at the site until spring on account of the difficulty and danger of landing material. Arrangements for the purchase of additional land were meantime being made; but it was not until the early part of June that the steps necessary to procure a clear title were concluded.

Unfortunately, it had been discovered that the 1878 act omitted necessary provisions for the land purchase and work had to be halted until such authority was obtained in June of 1880. Immediately thereafter, the Board reported, "An agreement was ...entered into with A.A. McCullough, of Norfolk, Va., for the building of the pier for landing material, and he is to complete the work by August 1 next, and guarantee its continuance for one year." The Board was at pains to show that, although nothing had really happened, the project was sure to be in full swing in the near future. "The materials for the concrete foundation have been purchased," the report noted,

The Light-House Board was anxious to complete a new light at Cape Henry when cracks in the old tower were detected. By early 1880, when this photo was taken, construction had begun, but it was December 1881 before the new light could be commissioned. Photo, The National Archives.

and will be shipped as soon as the construction-pier is in readiness to receive them. A concrete-mixer, to be operated by steam, has been constructed and transported to Norfolk, preparatory to its removal to the site. The sirens and boilers for the steam fog-signal...have been purchased, and the former delivered at Norfolk. An agreement for the furnishing of the brick-work for the fog-signal building has been entered into, and every measure looking toward a rapid and uninterrupted prosecution of the work is employed.

Unfortunately, however, all was not well.

The following year the Light-House Board complained that "[t]he work of rebuilding Cape Henry light-house was much delayed by the inability of the contractors to fulfill their contract for the iron-work..." There were additional problems with the newly constructed pier.

> *The temporary pier for landing material, commenced in the first week in July, was completed in August, as well as the laying of the tram-way and the erection of the hoisting apparatus. As soon as the arrangements for landing material were perfected, the broken stone for concrete, the hoisting-engines and steam concrete-mixer, 600 barrels of imperial Portland cement, brick for the fog-signal building and the fog-siren machinery, with the exception of the boilers, were landed. When the first cargo, 165 tons, of the tower iron-work had been placed on the pier and the hauling to the station commenced, the bridge leading to the pier broke with a loaded car on it.*

Examination of the wood revealed that it had been destroyed by a boring worm, *Teredo navalis* and that the same worm had eaten away the piles of the landing pier as well. A schooner was procured to remove the iron that had been unloaded on the bridge and take it to Norfolk where it could be temporarily stored. This proved a fortunate decision. "The work of removal," the Board reported, "commencing on September 16, was completed on the night of the 18th. The pier fell, the piles having been destroyed by the worm, at two o'clock on the morning of the 19th." It was decided that materials would thenceforth be transported by means of scows. When work on the lighthouse was once again suspended in November, the foundation excavation had been finished and filled with concrete to a depth of eight feet and the fog signal building, "a brick one-story structure, with one room 25 feet square for the engines and sirens, with shed attached...the whole covered with a galvanized, corrugated iron roof," had been completed. A workman—"properly housed," the Board reported—was left in charge of the property for the remainder of the winter.

On May 30th, 1881, a construction crew returned to the site and work proceeded relatively smoothly. "By the middle of June," the Board noted, "all the preparatory work, such as putting hoisting engines in order, erecting derricks, preparing cars for hauling, &c., [sic] had been completed. ....At the end of the month the concrete foundation, 11 feet in depth, was finished." Additionally, the contract for the metal work had been extended and was almost ready for shipment. "The work is now complete at the foundry," the Board reported, "with the exception of the fitting and finishing of the inside of the lantern and some minor work." Finally, the Board related that "a first-order lens for this station is on hand at the Staten Island depot and now ready for shipment. Unless unforeseen delays with the work occur it will be prosecuted till the final completion and lighting, which, it is hoped, can be done in the early winter."

On December 14, 1881, the light was taken from the old Cape Henry tower and placed in the newly constructed iron tower. The next day, the keeper assumed responsibility for the new first-order beacon and on the evening of December 15 a fixed white light with a fixed red sector, showing 157 feet above mean high water and visible at the time for 18³/₄ nautical miles, was officially placed in service.

The tower of the Cape Henry lighthouse, which marks the south side of the entrance to the Chesapeake Bay and is considered one of the most impor-

---

Light station established:
1791

Construction of present structure:
1881

Location:
On Cape Henry, seacoast of Virginia, south side of the entrance to the Chesapeake Bay.

Position:
36 55 35
76 00 27

Characteristic of light:
Active; Mo (U) white, 20-second interval; red sector from 154 to 233 degrees, covering shoals outside Cape Charles and Middle Ground inside bay.

Height of light, above mean high water:
157 feet.

Description of station:
Octagonal tower with a black base, service room, and lantern; shaft painted half white and half black on each face, alternating so that upper and lower halves of faces show alternately black and white.

Range:
White, 17 miles; red 15 miles.

Fog signal:
RACON: N (-.). Horn: 1 blast every 30 seconds (3-second blast), operating continuously.

Radio beacon:
CB (-.-. -...); range, 150 miles; frequency, 289kHz; antenna, 80 yards, 326 degrees, from Cape Henry light.

tant lighthouses on the Atlantic Coast, is also painted in one of the most distinctive patterns to be found on a lighthouse anywhere in the world. Each side of the octagonal tower is half white and half black in an alternating pattern of vertical stripes. All ships bound for Norfolk, Newport News, Baltimore and other Chesapeake Bay ports pass by the Cape Henry light. The height of the lighthouse from its base to the center of the lantern is 152 feet (170 feet from the base to the very top of the lantern's ventilator ball). The first-order Fresnel lens was originally outfitted with five concentric oil-burning wicks. In 1912 an incandescent oil-vapor lamp was installed. The red sector covered the shoals outside of Cape Charles and the Middle Ground that extend from the entrance into the Chesapeake Bay. In 1922 the characteristic of the Cape Henry light was changed from fixed white to a distinctive group-flashing light. The light station was outfitted with two bells that were simultaneously struck by machinery every five seconds.

In 1984, the new Cape Henry light was changed to unmanned operation and, within five years, the U.S. Coast Guard was exploring the prohibitive costs of maintaining the historical integrity of the structure and worrying about the bicentennial celebration of the United States lighthouse service which was to take place at the old Cape Henry light only a few hundred feet away. A memo directed by the commander of the Fifth Coast Guard District to the supervisor of the Cleveland Shore Maintenance Attachment was philosophical:

> *You informed us...that Cape Henry light, last painted in 1976, would not be painted this [fiscal year] due to prohibitive costs. You further recommended that we excess the structure and...build a skeleton tower for the required optic. We disagree with that approach. As the program manager, it is my decision to retain this lighthouse as one of the major landfall aids for the Chesapeake Bay entrance. A skeleton tower would not present the same visual daymark as the current 165-foot tower.*

"Politically," the memo continued,

> *it would be difficult to excess this light. ... The lack of adequate landmarks in the Chesapeake Bay approach necessitates the continued maintenance of this outstanding daymark, not a skeleton tower.*

The Fifth District commander requested that the shore maintenance detachment continue to arrange for structural repairs and "find a way to complete the paint job."

The work was not completed and discussion continued around six possible alternatives: 1) to follow the status quo—neither painting nor repairing the structure (cost: zero); 2) to remove the paint, sandblast and paint both the interior and exterior and repair all damaged metal work and sidewalks (cost: $302,000); 3) to paint only the exterior over the existing lead-based paint and make repairs to the metal work and sidewalks (cost: $311,000); 4) to turn over ownership of the lighthouse to a historical society and erect a maintenance-free tower near the existing lighthouse; 5) to turn over ownership of the lighthouse to a historical society to maintain the optic; and 6) to document and demolish the existing lighthouse and erect a maintenance-free tower. The supervisor of the Cleveland Shore Maintenance Detachment hoped that the fifth alternative could be worked out and he proposed to reach that goal by pursuing demolition. "To my knowledge," he wrote, "the Coast Guard is not funded to maintain historic structures... [but] I am confident that if we pursue alternative 6, and if preservation of Cape Henry light is a priority of this nation, that either a special interest group will come forward to assume maintenance... or Congress will authorize special funds to restore the light."

Fortunately, the commander of the Fifth District Headquarters in Portsmouth remained adamant: "Initiating action to demolish the existing Cape Henry light to erect a maintenance-free skeleton tower, or waiting for a special interest group to assume maintenance responsibility of

Over the years, Cape Henry light station has been the site of much experimentation with light, fog, radio and radar signals—and even, in the 1980's, with wind-generated electricity. Photo, The National Archives.

the light are avenues that will not work," he asserted. "Replacing this prominent landmark with a skeleton tower would be a severe operational, as well as political, miscalculation."

In 1990 the Association for the Preservation of Virginia Antiquities expressed an interest in leasing the new Cape Henry light. Meanwhile, however, major maintenance work remains to be done. In 1991, the Coast Guard spent $2,200 to repair fence posts and paint the fence surrounding the light, as well as to paint the entrance door, repair some cement steps, remove flaking paint from the radio beacon room and replace a cracked window.

Cape Charles

In 1827, Congress appropriated funds for the construction of the first Cape Charles lighthouse on the Lilliputian island, named for Captain John Smith, that lies just off the edge of Cape Charles at the entrance to the Chesapeake Bay. The lighthouse, 12 miles north by northeast of the Cape Henry light, marks the north side of the mouth of the Chesapeake Bay. Technically, Cape Charles is a seacoast light rather than a bay light. It was finished and commissioned in 1828, but there was immediate dissatisfaction with the light which, even under the most favorable conditions, could only be seen for 12 miles—a distance deemed inadequate for vessels approaching the cape from the Atlantic. The original lighthouse was a masonry tower, painted white, that stood 60 feet from its base to the lantern.

In its report to Congress in 1851, the special task force assigned to study and suggest improvements to the lighthouse service drew special attention to the inadequacy of the Cape Charles light and

Commissioned in 1883 to replace an 1828 tower, the Cape Charles light remains an important navigational aid. The original first-order Fresnel lens was replaced in 1963 when the light station was automated and the French-cut crystal lens is now on display at the Mariners' Museum in Newport News. Photo, U.S. Coast Guard.

recommended that an appropriation for the erection of a new tower be made as soon as possible and that the light be replaced with a first-order apparatus.

In the early 19th century, Cape Charles was a busy seaport. With the advent of the railroads, it also became an important junction for cargo bound for Norfolk and for passengers who were ferried between trains on the Pennsylvania Railroad's north-south line. Besides numerous maritime complaints about the light, the structure was threatened by the encroaching sea. In 1856, Congress appropriated $35,000 for the erection of a new tower. Although construction began the following year, it had only reached 83 feet when, in August of 1862, "the light was visited by a party of [Confederate] guerrillas, who completely destroyed the light, carrying away such portable articles as they deemed valuable." Construction materials collected at the site for the new tower were also plundered. Nevertheless, in 1864 an additional $20,000 was appropriated and a new 150-foot brick tower, white with a brown lantern and showing a flashing white light, was completed and exhibited on May 7 of that same year. The tower stood about one and one-quarter miles inland from the

Starke Jett

original lighthouse. It was placed under military guard for the remainder of the Civil War.

Over the next 20 years, shore erosion continued to threaten the masonry tower. By 1883 the water line was within 300 feet of the lighthouse and keeper's dwelling. Sea walls were constructed but the encroachment continued at the rate of 30 feet per year. Then, in 1889, a northeasterly storm washed away much of the protective timber and stone and temporarily surrounded the tower with water. New jetties were constructed but the lighthouse was condemned, and in December 1894, it was replaced with a white skeleton tower—built at a cost of $150,000—about one mile west of the second lighthouse. The light was first exhibited on August 15, 1895. (The condemned lighthouse tower stood until 1927 when it was washed away by a severe northeast storm.)

The new lighthouse—still an active light, though now 100 years old—is an octagonal, 191-foot pyramidal structure of cast iron with a concrete foundation and with spiral cast-iron steps enclosed in an iron column leading to the watch level. Until 1963, the lantern housed an enormous first-order crystal lens (manufactured in Paris by F. Barbier and Cie. in 1893)—a veritable glass house, six feet in diameter and 10 feet in height, containing hundreds of curved glass prisms held in place by polished brass plates. A small door on one side provided an entrance into the light. When the Coast Guard assumed responsibility for the station, a single foot-long, 1000-watt incandescent light bulb replaced the concentric circles of oil-burning wicks that were initially used to provide illumination.

The 16-sided lantern that housed the lens was constructed entirely of cast iron, including the balustrade, gallery deck, lantern floor and ventilator ball. A chamber directly beneath the lantern housed a small electric motor that rotated the light. The pedestal of the light floated in a cast-iron tub containing 300 pounds of mercury. A visitor to the light (shortly before it was dismantled and moved to the Mariners' Museum in 1963) noted that "the one-ton lens chamber is so precisely engineered and lubricated that the gentle pressure of a finger can cause it to rotate on its vertical axis."

The cast-iron work at the lantern and watch levels, though perfectly utilitarian in function, is also quite decorative. For example, the ceiling of the chamber beneath the lantern sports elegant cast-iron pediments which also provide structural support to the cupola and lantern deck above. Six brass ventilators were placed in the lower part of the lantern.

Until 1939, when the U.S. Coast Guard assumed administration of all navigational aids, the lighthouse was manned by civilian families—a keeper with a first and second assistant—who lived in three large homes built within 100 feet of the lighthouse. When the Coast Guard took over the light, its personnel served four days on the island and then had a two-day break. Most of their families lived off the island in the vicinity of Cape Charles. At night, the watch room was manned, as it was during storms, to ensure that the light remained lit.

During World War II three observation towers were installed in close proximity to the light by the U.S. Navy. From these vantage points, lookouts with high-powered binoculars searched the skies and the sea for enemy aircraft and U-boats and, in fact, several U-boats were spotted at the mouth of the Chesapeake Bay.

In 1963, the lighthouse was converted to automatic operation and the first-order Fresnel lens was replaced with 1.2 million candlepower DCB-24 searchlight with a visibility of 20 miles, similar to the beacons used in airports. In fact, the new light has no more visibility than the former beacon, but the Coast Guard was anxious to replace the light because the tub of mercury in which the original Fresnel lens was mounted vibrated in extreme weather, displacing the mercury and altering the position and performance of the light. The original light with all its machinery was estimated to weigh about three tons; the replacement light, including its base and rotating equipment weighed only 500 pounds. The Mariners' Museum in Newport News arranged with the Coast Guard to provide manpower to dismantle the Fresnel lens in exchange for ownership and the privilege of displaying it in the museum. When the Fifth Coast Guard District accepted the offer, the Mariners' Museum sent two trucks and six staff members to assist four coastguardsmen in carefully removing the lens and its machinery from the lantern in the 191-foot tower. The trucks were ferried, one at a time, across Smith Island Bay by a 52-foot scow. The museum curator found the prisms and machinery in excellent condition and discovered that the light parts were numbered, greatly facilitating reassembly in the museum. The sole damage to the prisms had been caused when a flock of geese flew into the tower during a storm, shattering the storm pane and chipping a few of the upper prisms of the lens. Besides this minimal damage, only the bolts and casings showed signs of corrosion.

In March 1989, the U.S. Coast Guard sent a maintenance crew to Smith Island. Ten days were spent in cleaning, scraping and repainting the entire structure to prevent further rust and corrosion. Cracked lantern panes were replaced and, when the renovation was completed, the Coast Guard reported the condition of Cape Charles light to be "very good."

Chesapeake Light—End of an Era

Technically a seacoast light, the United States Coast Guard commissioned the Chesapeake Off-Shore Light Structure to replace the Chesapeake light vessel on September 25, 1965. The Chesapeake lightship, a 133-foot ship built under the Lighthouse Service, had been placed in operation to mark the entrance to the Chesapeake Bay in 1933, but it was preceded by five other lightships—the first, No. 46, a steel, wood-sheathed sailing ship designed to withstand shocks and sudden temperature changes.

"Reasons of economy and stability," the Coast Guard noted proudly, "have dictated the replacement, but improved habitability is a factor which cannot be ignored." The light vessel required a crew of 15-18 whereas the tower initially was manned by six coastguardsmen, with four men at the station at all times. The box-like dwelling was built by the same company that constructed the Chesapeake Bay Bridge and Tunnel. It was prefabricated and barged to the site for assembly. An enormous crane was secured to a platform set in the sea bottom and used to lift the sections of the prefabricated building onto the Texas tower's foundation. The building, 75 feet above the sea, was designed with private accommodations for each member of the lighthouse crew and included six bedrooms, an oceanographic room, a radio station, a signal control and equipment room, a large generator room with small rooms for water storage, battery storage, heat and flammable storage, a galley and, according to newspaper accounts of the time, "a remarkably spacious recreational area." Transportation to and from the light station was by helicopter. Painted with two concentric circles, one with a 4-foot diameter, the other with a 20-foot diameter, the top of the building had been specifically designed to serve as a helicopter landing pad. The 11-foot-square, 37-foot-high light and instrument tower extends upward from one corner of the top deck. Beneath the living and working area, a storage facility for fuel and water was constructed, and beneath that, the lowest level housed a 25-foot fiberglass surfboat.

The last true lighthouse to be built on the bay, Chesapeake Light, commissioned in 1965, features a helicopter landing pad and spacious living quarters for six lightkeepers. It was placed on unmanned operation in 1989—though many local residents will swear that it is manned. Photo, U.S. Coast Guard.

The blue "Texas tower" was constructed 14½ miles east of Cape Henry (13 nautical miles from the coastline of Virginia Beach). The stark skeletal structure is supported by specially constructed corrosion-resistant steel pilings, painted black. The pilings are 33 inches in diameter, driven 180 feet into the ocean floor, and filled with reinforced concrete. The height of the structure, from the bottom of the pilings to the tower light, is upwards of 400 feet. On two sides of the platform, ladders and boat hoists were constructed for boat-landing operations.

As a navigational aid, the Chesapeake light station incorporated the newest technology, both with respect to the light and with respect to its fog signal and radio beacon. "The main light," the Coast Guard reported, "which is a highly advanced engineering prototype, utilizing a glass tube filled with xenon gas, can be seen at a distance of 16 miles. It is rated at 6,000,000 candle power for high intensity operation, with provisions for reduced operation at 600,000 candle power." The Coast Guard noted that the use of xenon flash arrays reduced the consumption of electrical power and that it was directed by "simple reflective arrays, rather than the expensive and fragile prismatic lenses" required in conventional lights. The fog signal was designed to have a 10-mile range and the tower's radio beacon a range of 70 miles.

Fifteen years later, in March of 1980, plans for the complete automation of the light station were drawn up. The Coast Guard justified the automation by noting that the project would "eliminate isolated duty" for six military personnel "while still maintaining an aid to navigation that will meet the needs of the mariner."

There were three phases to the automation, each lasting two months. In May and June of 1980 the automatic equipment was installed and tested, including the navigation signal equipment with its remote control and monitoring systems, the radio transmitting and receiving equipment, antennas, and the fire-protection system. This was described by the Coast Guard as a "manned-automated" mode of operating.

During Phase II, the automation power room was built and the automation equipment was placed on 10KW engine generators. Two of the three 40KW engine generators were removed; the other was left for personnel requirements. The station was now completely automated though still manned.

Finally, during Phase III (September and October 1980) the windows were secured, security latches were installed and all excess equipment was removed to reduce the load on the tower legs (and, it was hoped, to thereby increase the light's structural safety). When the interior of the light station was reworked, two bunk rooms were designed as emergency quarters for maintenance crews. Additionally, emergency rations and water were maintained at the station and the remaining 40KW engine generator was left behind for use when maintenance crews boarded the structure.

Maintenance plans for the light were also drawn up. Noting that the light was scheduled for painting in 1989, the Coast Guard engineers estimated that the coating would last for 15 years. "At the end of 10 years," they stated, "the paint condition will be evaluated, the tower recaulked, and the helicopter deck resurfaced. No internal painting will be required."

The light station continues to be serviced by the U.S. Coast Guard and is occasionally used by other groups, such as civilian and military personnel from the U.S. Naval Air Warfare Center, who have camped on the station to record dogfights on electronic videos. Most of these guests, the Coast Guard reports, are well behaved. In the summer of 1993, however, a group using the light threw a water balloon on a boater and damaged his radio. The next day another boater took pictures while the galley cook jettisoned garbage containing plastic materials from the light. The Coast Guard moved quickly to ensure that such incidents would not reoccur by tightening procedures surrounding the light station's use by non-Coast Guard groups.

Light station established:
1933

Construction of present structure:
1965

Location:
Fourteen and one-half miles east of Cape Henry (13 nautical miles from the coastline of Virginia Beach).

Position:
36 54.3
74 42.8

Characteristic of light:
Flashing (2) white, 15-second interval.

Height of light, above mean high water:
117 feet.

Range:
24 miles.

Description of station:
Blue tower on white square superstructure on four black piles. CHESAPEAKE painted on the sides.

Fog signal:
Horn: 1 blast every 30 seconds (3-second blast), operating continuously.
RACON: N (-.).

Bibliography

Abell, Shirley. "A Gleam Across the Waves for the Men at Sea," *The Baltimore Evening Sun*, March 11, 1943.

Adams, William Henry Davenport. *Lighthouses and Lightships: A Descriptive and Historical Account of their Mode of Construction and Organization*. T. Nelson and Sons, 1870.

Adamson, Hans Christian. *Keepers of the Lights*. New York: Greenberg Publisher, 1955.

Ainsley, Mary Jeanne. "Bay Light: Welcome...Warning...," *Virginia Maritimer*, September 1986.

"Alight Again," *The Gazette Packet*, November 4, 1993.

"Baltimore Light First Atomic-Powered," *The Baltimore Sun*, June, 1964.

"Baltimore, Then and Now," *The Baltimore American*, August 22, 1954.

Barrow, Mary Reid. "The Guiding Light," clipping from U.S. Coast Guard 5th District Headquarters' files with no citation.

Bates, Steve. "Jones Point Light Flashes Back On," *The Washington Post*, October 30, 1993.

"Bay Lighthouse Explodes; Two Attendants Escape," *The Baltimore Evening Sun*, April 30, 1960.

"Beacon on the Bay," *The Baltimore News-American*, July 18, 1979.

Beattle, Heather. "Vandalism at New Point Lighthouse Continuing," *The Gloucester-Mathews Gazette-Journal*, July 14, 1994.

Bilek, Babette. "The Ghosts of Pt. Lookout Light," *Maryland Magazine*, State of Maryland, Summer, 1984.

Blitz, John. "Coast Guard Crew Has Civilian Boss, *The Baltimore Evening Sun*, December 16, 1965.

Bonko, Larry. "Light Source Varied Over Years," *The Virginian-Pilot*, July 31, 1969.

Bowen, Perry Gray, Jr. Notes from a talk given by Perry Gray Bowen, Jr. to The Calvert County Historical Society, January 19, 1990.

Brown, Alexander Crosby. "Wolf Trap Shoal," *Chesapeake Skipper*, April, 1951.

Burgess, Robert H. "Lightship at Bay's Mouth Serving Its Last Days," *The Baltimore Sun*, September 12, 1965.

Calvert Marine Museum. A History of Drum Point Lighthouse. *Calvert Marine Museum, Special Publication No. 1*, 1980 (c. 1976).

Chesapeake Bay Lighthouses. The Maryland Historic Trust and Gredell & Associates, Structural Engineers, September, 1991.

Clarke, Wendy Mitman. "Jones Point Lighthouse To Shine Again," *Soundings*, July, 1993.

Clarke, Wendy Mitman. "Lighthouse Shines Again," *Soundings*, January, 1994.

"Coast Guard Offers Reward," *Soundings*, August 2, 1976.

Cronin, William B. "The Chesapeake Bay's Endangered Lighthouses," *Maryland Magazine*, State of Maryland, Summer, 1990.

de Gast, Robert. *The Lighthouses of the Chesapeake*, Baltimore, Maryland: Johns Hopkins University Press, 1973.

Department of Commerce and Labor, Bureau of Lighthouses, U.S. Commissioner of Lighthouses. *Annual Reports*. Washington, D.C.: U.S. Gov. Printing Office, 1910-1939.

Department of Commerce and Labor, U.S. Lighthouse Establishment. *Specifications and Contract for Erection of Baltimore Light-House*, 1906.

Department of Transportation, U.S. Coast Guard. *Historically Famous Lighthouses*. Washington, D.C.: U.S. Government Printing Office,1957.

Department of Transportation, U.S. Coast Guard. *Light List, Volume II, Atlantic Coast*. Washington, D.C.: U.S. Government Printing Office, 1994.

Department of the Treasury, Office of the U.S. Light-House Board. *Annual Reports*. Washington, D.C.: U.S. Government Printing Office, 1852-1910.

Department of the Treasury, Office of the U.S. Light-House Board. *List of Lights and Fog Signals of the Atlantic and Gulf Coasts of the United States*. Washington, D.C.: U.S. Government Printing Office, 1896.

Di Vincenzo, Mark. "Battered Beacon Gets A Facelift," *The Daily Press*, May 19, 1991.

Dorsey, Jack. "Old Cape Henry Lighthouse May Gleam as Beach Signal," *The Ledger-Star*, August 26, 1965.

Dulaney, Carroll. Column appearing in *The Baltimore News-Post*, February 28, 1936.

Easley, Owen. "Cape Charles Lighthouse Goes Automatic," *The Ledger-Star*, November 16, 1963.

Evans, Philip E. "One of Maryland's Last Manned Lighthouses," *The Baltimore Sun*, March 18, 1962.

Ewalt, Anna Weems. "Grandparents Living in a Lighthouse," *The Baltimore Sun Magazine*, November 18, 1979.

Goyette, Barbara. "Lighthouse Lift," *Chesapeake Bay Magazine*, January, 1989.

133

Hardy, Spencer. "For the Last Time—Grandma Trims the Lamp," *The New York Mirror*, December 7, 1947.

Hatch, Charles E., Jr. "The Old Cape Henry Light: A Survey Report," unpublished report, Colonial National Historic Park, February, 1962.

Henderson, Randi. "O'Neill's Heroism Wins Lighthouse," *The Baltimore Sun*, November 9, 1977.

Holland, Francis Ross, Jr. *America's Lighthouses: An Illustrated History*. New York: Dover Publications, 1988 (c. 1972).

"Ice Again Delays Shipping in Port," *The Baltimore Sun*, February 19, 1936.

"In Dark Times He Keeps A Bright Spot For Mariners on the Bay," *The Baltimore Evening Sun*, ca. 1940.

Johnson, Arnold B. *The Modern Lighthouse Service*. Washington, D.C.: U.S. Government Printing Office, 1890.

Joynes, J. William. "Lighthouse Keeping," *The Baltimore American*, June 19, 1955.

Klein, Donald. "Texas Towers Due to Replace Picturesque Lightship Landmark," *The Baltimore Evening Sun*, August 9, 1960.

Kryziwicki, Fran. "Bay Lights Are Dimming: Beacons Falling Victim to Vandals, Thieves," *The Washington Post*, August 6, 1979.

"Lighthouse is Automatic," *The Baltimore Sun*, May 7, 1948.

"Lighthouse Nuclear Unit Due Tests," *The Baltimore Evening Sun*, January 16, 1963.

"Lighthouse to be U.S. Landmark," *The Virginian-Pilot*, May 2, 1964.

Little, J.G., II, and Harvard Ayers. *Notes and Comments on the Archaeology of a Late Nineteenth and Early Twentieth Century Light House on Jones Point, Alexandria, Virginia*. Prepared for the National Park Service, Department of Anthropology, The Catholic University of America, Washington, D.C., 1967.

Mays, Jim. "Horizontal Ladder to Success," *The Virginian-Pilot*, October 28, 1965.

McAllen, William. "Saga of a Lighthouse," *Maryland Magazine*, State of Maryland, Spring, 1989.

Melville, Greg. "Jones Point Lighthouse To Welcome Travelers Once More," *The Gazette Packet*, October 28, 1993.

Mighall, Mark L., as told to Bob Liston. "'Flames Were All Around Us,' Says Lighthouse Tender," *The Baltimore American*, May 1, 1960.

Moberly, Elizabeth H. "Tom White's Lighthouse Out in the Chesapeake Can Be A Far Cry from the Place of Peace and Quiet You Might Suppose," *The Baltimore Sun*, October 31, 1948.

"More Bay Lights Going Automatic," *The Baltimore Sun*, April 6, 1960.

"Moving Day After 92 Years," *The Baltimore Evening Sun*, April 1, 1975.

Mulford, Ralph E. "Light Keepers Unruffled," *The Virginian-Pilot*, April 16, 1960.

Noble, Dennis L. and Ralph E. Eshelman. "A Lighthouse for Drum Point," *The Keeper's Log*, Summer, 1987.

Nordhoff, Charles, "The Lighthouses of the United States," *Harper's Weekly Magazine*, Vol. 38, March, 1874.

Norris, Joseph. "Piney Point Lighthouse Museum Open to Public After Refurbishing," *Finer Points: Quarterly Newsletter of the St. Clement's Island-Potomac River Museum*, Summer, 1994.

"Nuclear Reactor To Run Baltimore Light," *The Baltimore Evening Sun*, May 20, 1964.

Office of the Light-House Board. *Laws of the United States Relating to the Establishment, Support, and Management of the Light-Houses, Light-Vessels, Monuments, Beacons, Spindles, Buoys, and Public Piers of the United States, August 7, 1789 to March 3, 1855*. Washington: A.O.P. Nicholson, Public Printer, 1855.

Oman, Anne H. "Ups and Downs, All Around," *The Washington Post Weekend*, August 19, 1983.

Putnam, George R. *Lighthouses and Lightships of the United States*. Boston: Houghton Mifflin Co., 1917.

Roberts, Bruce, and Ray Jones. *Southern Lighthouses*. Chester, Connecticut: Globe Pequot Press, 1989.

"She Does Lighthouse Keeping, "*The Baltimore Evening Sun*, July 15, 1938.

Smith, John. *Generall Historie of Virginia, New-England, and the Summer Isles*. Selections. Bobbs-Merrill, 1970.

Smith, Mary Wade. "Wolf Trap Light Has Stood Through the Years as Mariners Guide in Chesapeake," *The Gloucester Gazette-Journal*, August 6, 1964.

Stevenson, John. "Cape Henry Lighthouse Lit by Wind," *The Virginian-Pilot*, March 5, 1982.

Taylor, Craig E. "Lighthouse Keeping," *The Baltimore Sun*, October 13, 1946.

Tilp, Frederick. "Jones Point Lighthouse," uncited article in files of the Chesapeake Chapter, U.S. Lighthouse Society.

The Friends of Concord Point Lighthouse and The Maryland Historical Trust. *Historic Structures Report: Keeper's House, Concord Point Lighthouse*. Prepared by Clio Group, Inc. and John M. Adams, Architect, 1990.

Record Group No. 26. *Records of the U.S. Coast Guard and its predecessors, The Bureau of Lighthouses and the U.S. Light-House Board*. The National Archives of the United States, Washington, D.C.

Ullman, William. "Lighthouse Folk Celebrate 150 Years," *The Baltimore Sun*, July 2, 1939.

U.S. Lighthouse Establishment. *Compilation of Public Documents and Extracts from Reports and Papers Relating to Light-Houses, Light-Vessels, and Illuminating Apparatus, and to Beacons, Buoys and Fog Signals*, 1789 to 1871. Washington: Government Printing Office, 1871.

U.S. Coast Guard. "Histories of Wolf Trap Light Vessel and Lighthouse, " report in the files of the U.S. Coast Guard 5th District Headquarters, Portsmouth, Virginia (n. d.).

U.S. Coast Guard. "New Point Comfort Light Station," report in the files of the U.S. Coast Guard 5th District Headquarters, Portsmouth, Virginia (n. d.).

Ward, Jane. *Hooper Strait Lighthouse.* J & J Ward, 1986 (c. 1979).

Wentzel, Michael. "Life of Lighthouse Keeper Was Not Boring for John," *The Evening Sun*, August 20, 1983.

Weiss, George. *The Lighthouse Service: Its History, Activities and Organizations*. Baltimore, Maryland: The Johns Hopkins Community Press, 1926.

Wilson, Randy. "Vandals Hit Lighthouse," *The Baltimore News-American*, July 18, 1979.

Wilson, Woodrow T. "Keeper of Solomon's Lump Light," *The Crisfield Times*, December 20, 1974.

Note: In addition to the articles and books cited, the author has relied on interviews and conversations with many individuals and archival material available at The Archives of the United States, Washington, D.C.; The U.S. Coast Guard Headquarters, Washington, D.C.; The U.S. Coast Guard 5th District Headquarters, Portsmouth, Virginia; The Enoch Pratt Library, Baltimore, Maryland; The Library of Congress, Washington, D.C.; The Chesapeake Bay Maritime Museum, St. Michaels, Maryland; and The Calvert Marine Museum, Solomons, Maryland.

Index